I0114789

COMMERCIALISATION
AND PRIVATISATION
OF OUTER SPACE
Issues for National Space Legislation

Edited by

Prof. (Dr.) R. Venkata Rao

Vice-Chancellor,
National Law School of India University, Bangalore

Mr. Kumar Abhijeet

Assistant Professor,
National Law School of India University, Bangalore

KW
KNOWLEDGE WORLD

KW Publishers Pvt Ltd
New Delhi

Copyright © 2016
R. Venkata Rao and Kumar Abhijeet

All rights reserved. No part of this publication may be reproduced, stored in a retrieval system, or transmitted in any form or by any means, electronic, mechanical, photocopying, recording or otherwise, without the prior written permission of the copyright owner.

ISBN   978-93-83649-86-0

Published in India by Kalpana Shukla

KW
KNOWLEDGE WORLD

KW Publishers Pvt Ltd
4676/21, First Floor, Ansari Road, Daryaganj, New Delhi 110002
Phone: +91 11 23263498/43528107
Email: knowledgeworld@vsnl.net • www.kwpub.com

2011   **F P / B A**   BEST PUBLISHERS AWARD (ENGLISH)

Printed and Bound in India

Contents

Brief Comments

Annexures

Acknowledgements

Since the genesis of this book is owed to the round table conference on space law held on July 18, 2015, it is important to acknowledge and express our thanks to all those who joined hands with us to make this event a successful one. We express our deepest gratitude to Hon'ble Justice Mr. Raghvendra S. Chauhan, Judge High Court of Karnataka, the Chief Guest for valedictory function, for sparing his precious time to be with us throughout the conference right from the inauguration. We are equally indebted to Hon'ble Dr. M. Y. S. Prasad, former Director, Satish Dhawan Space Centre (SHAR), Sriharikota and Chairman, National Space Law Committee of ISRO. Dr. Prasad was generous enough to spend almost half a day with us which was very encouraging.

Hon'ble Dr. G. Madhavan Nair, President International Academy of Astronautics and former Chairman ISRO, filled our heart with joy by coming all the way from Thiruvananthapuram to inaugurate the conference. We express our heartfelt thanks to him for gracing the inaugural session with his benign presence.

We are overwhelmed to receive a message from Dr. Jitendra Singh, Hon'ble Minister of State (Independent Charge), Department of Space. Our deepest gratitude to the Hon'ble Minister.

We do not have words to thank Prof. (Dr.) Stephan Hobe, Director, Institute of Air and Space Law who despite his busy schedule managed time through video-conferencing. Prof. Hobe is an ardent and learned scholar in the filed of space law. His esteemed plenary address revealed the contours of national space legislation, the demands of international law and how it is implemented.

This conference would have been meaningless but for the learned resource persons travelling from different parts of the country to NLSIU Bangalore. Our heart felt thanks to Prof. K. R. Sridhara Murthy, Vice-President International Institute of Space Law; Prof. Balakista Reddy, Head, Centre for Air and Space Law, NALSAR, Hyderabad and Dr. Ranjana Kaul who enthusiastically extended their full cooperation and not only shared their esteemed thoughts on the topic in discussion but also chaired the sessions of the conference.

The esteemed resource persons Dr. G. S. Sachdeva, Dr. Sandeep Bhat, Mr. Govindarajan, Dr. Susmita Mohanty, Mr. Ashok, Mr. Prashant, Mr. Narayan Prasad were outstanding. The stimulating discussions channelised by Mr. K. Krishna, Dr. Malay, Mr. Prateep, Mr. Pulkit, Mr. Deva Prasad and many other steamed up in the right direction. Our sincere thanks to all of them. We appreciate Dr. Saligram Bhatt, a pioneering scholar in the filed of air and space law for sending his paper and comment in absentia.

It was motivating for us to find like-minded people from different parts of the country volunteering to join hands with us. We had participants from our own Karnataka to the Capital of India; from Bengal sweets to the glamorous Mumbai. Our heartiest thanks to each one of them for making it to NLSIU B'lore.

When we organise any event, its success depends ultimately on all those people who had worked in planning and organising both the technical programme and in supporting the social arrangements. We would like to extend our heartiest appreciation to all the members of the NLSIU family— both teaching and non-teaching.

We will fail in our duty if we do not thank the sponsor for our event–TMT Law Practice, New Delhi. Our special thanks to Mr. Abhishek Malhotra, Managing Partner TMT Law Practice, New Delhi.

Once again, we thank all the distinguished guests, esteemed resource persons, participants, NLSIU family members and all those whom we might have missed incidentally but not intentionally.

The various researched papers published in this book would not have been possible but for the cooperation received from the respective contributors. Our sincere thanks to each one of them. Profuse thanks to Ms. Kalpana Shukla and Mr. Jose Mathew from KW Publishers Pvt. Ltd. for their sincere efforts in the publication of this book.

Editors

About the Editors

Prof. (Dr.) R. Venkata Rao

Prof. (Dr.) R. Venkata Rao, is a Professor of Law and Vice-Chancellor at the National Law School of India University, Bangalore.

Prof. Rao's academic qualifications are BA (Hons.) Litt, MA (Litt), ML and PhD. He has the distinction of receiving the Best Teacher Award from the Government of Andhra Pradesh in 2006; the Best Researcher Award from the Andhra University in 2003 and a Gold Medal for the Best PhD Thesis. He has been awarded the "Best Vice Chancellor Award for Outstanding Contribution to Education" during the World Chancellors and Vice Chancellor's Congress 2014 held on June 27, 2014 at Mumbai.

He has published more than 120 papers in the journals of national and international repute, apart from presenting numerous papers at various national and international seminars. He has guided successfully 1 LLD, 16 PhDs. and more than 75 M.Phil scholars.

He has served for 31 years in the Faculty of Law, Andhra University in various capacities as the Dean, Faculty of Law; Principal, University College of Law; Chairman, Board of Studies in Law and Head of the Department of Law; Dean of Student's Affairs, Andhra University.

Prof. Rao has been associated with several prestigious bodies like the Union Public Service Commission (UPSC), New Delhi; the University Grants Commission (UGC), New Delhi; National Assessment and Accreditation Council (NAAC), Bangalore; several Ministries in the Government of India and several Universities in India and abroad as an expert in various committees. He has also served as the Vice President, Indian Society of International Law, New Delhi and is a member of the executive and academic councils of a number of Universities.

Kumar Abhijeet

Mr. Kumar Abhijeet is Assistant Professor at the National Law School of India University, Bangalore. He is also a research scholar at the Institute of Air and Space Law, University of Cologne, Germany.

Mr. Abhijeet's academic qualification is BSc (Hons), University of Delhi; LLB Faculty of Law, University of Delhi; PG Diploma in

International Trade Law, Indian Law Institute, Delhi; LLM, National Law School of India University, Bangalore. He was a recipient of the Linnaeus–Palme fellowship, an exchange student to the *Kungliga Tekniska Hogskolon* (Royal Institute of Technology) Stockholm, Sweden. He did part of his LLM studies and Masters' thesis at this Institute. As a recipient of the Erasmus Mundus fellowship, he was a Visiting Scholar at the Department of Public International Law, Gent University, Belgium.

He has participated and presented papers at a number of national and international conferences. He was awarded twice for best paper presentation at two distinct international conferences. He has a few publications to his credit. He is member of the International Institute of Space Law. He is keen on the study of impact of science and technology on the society.

Mr. Kumar Abhijeet was the coordinator of the roundtable conference on "Commercialization and Privatization of Outer Space: Issues for National Space Legislation" held on July 18, 2015, organized by the National Law School of India University, Bangalore, in association with TMT Law Practice, New Delhi, at NLSIU, Bangalore.

About the Contributors

V. Balakista Reddy

Dr. V. Balakista Reddy, is Professor of International Law; Course Director, LLM International Trade and Business Laws (ITBL); Coordinator M.K. Nambyar SAARC Law Center and Head, Center for Air and Space Law, NALSAR University of Law, Hyderabad. Dr. Reddy obtained his LLM in International Law from the Osmania University and M.Phil. and Ph.D. in International Air and Space Law from the Jawaharlal Nehru University (JNU), New Delhi. He has more than 14 years of teaching and research experience. Currently, Prof. Reddy is also the Registrar of the NALSAR University, Hyderabad.

An internationally recognised expert in Air and Space Law, Dr. Reddy has also participated and presented papers in many national and international conferences and workshops including the UN conferences.

A prolific writer, Dr. Reddy has contributed extensively to the various national and international journals on the different facets of International law. Has has authored few books as well and has supervised M.Phil. and Ph.D. students.

He is also a visiting faculty to the Asian Institute of Transport Development, the Indian Society of International Law, the Foundation for Aviation & Sustainable Tourism and the National Institute of Aviation Management and Research, New Delhi, the Administrative Staff College of India and the Indo-American Centre for International Studies (formerly ASRC), Hyderabad. He is also an active member of many professional institutions including the Indian Society of International Law (ISIL) and the Aeronautical Society of India (AeSI), New Delhi.

Susmita Mohanty

Susmita Mohanty is a spaceship designer and aerospace entrepreneur. Ms. Mohanty is the co-founder and CEO of EARTH2ORBIT, India's first private space start-up. She has co-founded and led two other companies, MOONFRONT in San Francisco [2001–2007] and LIQUIFER in Vienna [2004–ongoing]. Before turning entrepreneur, Susmita worked in business development for the International Space Station programme at Boeing in

California. She also worked on the Shuttle-Mir missions at NASA's Johnson Space Center in Houston. Since 1998, she has worked with the Americans, Japanese, Europeans, Russians and Indians in various capacities—as employee, consultant, contractor, entrepreneur and advisor. In 2005, she was honoured on the Capitol Hill [Washington DC] with the International Achievement Award for promoting international cooperation through entrepreneurial space ventures. In 2012, she was voted into the *Financial Times'* list of "25 Indians to Watch". Educated in India, France and Sweden, Susmita holds multiple degrees including a PhD.

Stephan Hobe

Prof. (Dr.) Stephan Hobe is the Director of the Institute of Air and Space Law, the University of Cologne, Germany. He is also holder of the Jean-Monnet Chair for International and European Law, the University of Cologne, Germany and the Managing Director of the International Investment Law Centre Cologne (IILCC).

Prof. Hobe's academic qualifications are LLM, McGill University (Montreal, Canada); Doctor juris (Kiel). He has more than 250 publications to his credit. He is the editor of the *German Journal of Air and Space Law* (ZLW) and of the Series "Studies in Air and Space Law"; He has co-edited a number of books including the award-winning *Cologne Commentary on Space Law* which runs into over three volumes.

He has received the Distinguished Service Award (2009) of the International Institute of Space Law; was awarded (2010) by the International Academy of Astronautics for the best book of the year (*Cologne Commentary on Space Law, Vol. 1*); awarded (2013) by the University of Cologne for distinguished teaching; received the 2014 Prize of the International Academy of Astronautics, Social Class for the book *Pioneers of Space Law*.

He holds a number of honorary positions like full member International Academy of Astronautics; Rapporteur of Space Law Committee, International Law Association; Board of Directors, International Institute of Space Law; Member of the Advisory Board, German Society of International Law, Member American Society of International Law and many others.

Sridhara Murthi

Mr. Sridhara Murthi is the Vice-President of the International Institute of Space Law; Adjunct Professor, Jain University and Adjunct Faculty, National Institute of Advanced Studies.

Mr. Murthi is a leading expert in space commercialisation and space policy with his rich experience in India's space programme in key positions.

He has served as the Managing Director of the Antrix Corporation, and also as the Scientific Secretary of the Indian space agency, ISRO. He has extensively contributed to the technology transfer and space industry development programmes in the ISRO and also served as a counsellor at the Embassy of India in Paris, promoting cooperation between the space agencies/industry from Europe and India's space establishments. Mr. Murthi has a rich experience in the promotion of international cooperation in the peaceful uses of outer space.

He was elected as the Vice President of the International Astronautical Federation during 1998–2002, responsible for relations with the international organisations. He represented India as a delegate to the United Nations Committee on Peaceful Uses of Outer Space. He is the Vice President of the International Institute of Space Law (IISL) and a Trustee of the International Academy of Astronautics (IAA). He has been the recipient of the Social Sciences Award of the International Academy of Astronautics in 2003; the Astronautical Society of India Award in Space Systems Management in 2004; the ISRO Merit Award in 2007 for Commercialization and the Lifetime Achievement Award from the International Institute of Space Law in 2007.

He has around forty publications in national and international journals and is the co-editor of the book, *Perspectives in Communications*, published by the World Scientific Publishing Company, Singapore.

Sandeepa Bhat B.

Dr. Sandeepa Bhat is working as Associate Professor (Law) at the National University of Juridical Sciences (NUJS), Kolkata. He is the Coordinator for the Forum on Air and Space Law, NUJS, Kolkata and he also coordinates the Post Graduate Diploma in Air and Space Law.

He has more than eleven years of teaching and research experience at the National Law School of India University (NLSIU), Bangalore and the NUJS, Kolkata. He did his LLB from the Mangalore University with third rank and a gold medal. He has done his specialisation in International Law and Business and Trade Law (LLM) with first rank and double gold medal at the University of Mysore. His Ph.D. is in the field of Space Law.

Dr. Bhat has the experience of researching on the World Bank's Major research project on public health laws and regulations and the Indian Space

Research Organization (ISRO)'s major research project on laws relating to satellite financing. He has the distinction of being a member of the International Institute of Space Law (IISL), Paris, France.

Dr. Bhat is the founding Editor-in-Chief of the *Asian Journal of Air and Space Law* and is also associated with various other publications in different capacities. He has edited two books on space law and has published more than twenty-five articles in the various journals of international and national repute. He has presented more than twenty research papers at international and national conferences including the coveted International Astronautical Congress, IISL, and the ISIL International Conference on the Law of Outer Space (Jakarta, Indonesia).

Saligram Bhatt

Prof. Saligram Bhatt is currently Adjunct Prof. of Law at the NALSAR University and the ITM University Law School, Gurgaon, Haryana, India.

Dr. Bhatt is a Post-Doctoral Fulbright Research Scholar in Air Law, Space Law and Environment Law, School of Law, the Southern Methodist University, Dallas, Texas, USA, 1969–1970. He has a Ph.D. in International Law from the Jawaharlal Nehru University, with in specialisation in Air Law and Space Law under the guidance of Dr. Nagendra Singh, Judge of the ICJ. Dr. Bhatt has more than forty years of extensive experience in civil aviation administration, legal/policy matters, drafting or amending of primary aviation legislation and detailed civil aviation regulations, etc. for the Director General Civil Aviation (DGCA), Govt. of India, with the ICAO and other aviation-related organisations. He was the Director of Air Transport Regulations and the Deputy Director General of Civil Aviation, Govt. of India (1984–1988), Chairman, National Facilitation of Passengers Committee in DGCA and has drafted air laws and policy briefs for the Government of India.

As a Member of the Air Delegation, Government of India, he has participated in about 60 Government of India negotiations with the foreign governments for the drafting of air agreements and for making briefs for Air India and Indian Airlines. In this position, he has negotiated with the governments of numerous countries including the UK, USA, Canada, China, the former USSR, Gulf countries, African countries, countries in Southeast Asia, Pakistan, Sri Lanka, Bangladesh and Afghanistan. Dr. Bhatt was Adviser/Consultant to the United Nations (ICAO) on civil aviation for the Governments of Botswana, and Somalia on Airports Infrastructure, Air Space Management and Air Transport Regulations. He was instrumental in drafting the bilateral air agreements of Botswana with several countries like South Africa, Namibia, Zambia, etc.

Prof. Bhatt was an Honorary Professor of International Law (Emeritus level) of Air and Space Law, Jawaharlal Nehru University, New Delhi and Honorary Professor, Centre for Federal Studies, Jamia Hamdard University, New Delhi.

He has authored a number of books and has numerous publications to his credit.

Ranjana Kaul

Dr. Ranjana Kaul is Partner in Dua Associates and practices law in New Delhi.

Dr. Kaul's practice has included advocacy at the High Court of Delhi as Counsel for the Union of India and at the Supreme Court of India as Counsel for the State of Maharashtra. Her legal consultancy practice is in the area of corporate and commercial law including contracts, foreign exchange regulations, company law, IPR laws, related procedure law as well as close coordination with the relevant government agencies.

She has LLM degree from the Institute of Air and Space Law, McGill University, Canada; received her law degree from the University of Delhi and doctorate from the University of Puna.

She has number of publications to her credit and has been invited as a speaker to a number of national and internal conferences.

Prateep Basu

Based in Bangalore, Mr. Prateep Basu joined the Northern Sky Research, a global market research and consulting firm in space industry in the year 2014 after completing his 'Masters in Science' from the International Space University (ISU), Strasbourg, in the area of 'Space Studies'. His area of work at the NSR includes satellite manufacturing, launch services, UAVs, and earth-observation markets. Prior to attending the ISU, Mr. Basu had a two-year term with the Indian Space Research Organization (ISRO) as an engineer at the spaceport of Sriharikota, where he worked on six launch missions of the PSLV, and as a project engineer for the GLSV MK-III fluid mock-up. He has also worked closely with the ISRO as an intern in the areas of launch vehicle engineering and business development at various centres like the Vikram Sarabhai Space Centre (VSSC), the Liquid Propulsion System Centre (LPSC) and the commercial wing of the ISRO, Antrix, while pursuing his 'Bachelors in Technology' in the field of 'Aerospace Engineering' from the Indian Institute of Space Science and Technology (IIST), Thiruvananthapuram.

Mr. Basu has published his research in reputed international journals and conferences on subject such as diverse as computational fluid dynamics, space policy, climate change and liquid propulsion engineering. He is passionate about working towards sustainable commercial space business models that will drive social entrepreneurship and economic development.

Narayan Prasad

Mr. Narayan Prasad is the Managing Director and co-founder of Dhruva Space, a Bengaluru-based new space company established in 2012 with a vision to lead the turnkey small satellite development industry in India. He is an EGIDE scholar, Erasmus Mundus Space Master graduate and the curator of New Space India who is currently analysing technology, economic and policy models of India for a New Space revolution.

Malaya Adhikari

Dr. Malaya Adhikari is Assistant Professor of Law at Alliance University, Bangalore.

His academic qualification is Ph.D. (Jawaharlal Nehru University, New Delhi); M.Phil. Space Law (NALSAR, Hyderabad); LLM (International Law) and M.Sc. (Physics).

Dr. Adhikari has participated and presented papers at a number of national and international conferences. He has a few publications to his credit.

Kumar Abhijeet

Mr. Kumar Abhijeet is Assistant Professor at the National Law School of India University, Bangalore. He is also a research scholar at the Institute of Air and Space Law, University of Cologne, Germany.

Mr. Abhijeet's academic qualification is BSc (Hons), University of Delhi; LLB Faculty of Law, University of Delhi; PG Diploma in International Trade Law, Indian Law Institute, Delhi; LLM, National Law School of India University, Bangalore. He was a recipient of the Linnaeus–Palme fellowship, an exchange student to the *Kungliga Tekniska Hogskolon*

(Royal Institute of Technology) Stockholm, Sweden. He did part of his LLM studies and Masters' thesis at this Institute. As a recipient of the Erasmus Mundus fellowship, he was a Visiting Scholar at the Department of Public International Law, Gent University, Belgium.

He has participated and presented papers at a number of national and international conferences. He was awarded twice for best paper presentation at two distinct international conferences. He has a few publications to his credit. He is member of the International Institute of Space Law. He is keen on the study of impact of science and technology on the society.

Mr. Kumar Abhijeet was the coordinator of the roundtable conference on "Commercialization and Privatization of Outer Space: Issues for National Space Legislation" held on July 18, 2015, organized by the National Law School of India University, Bangalore, in association with TMT Law Practice, New Delhi, at NLSIU, Bangalore.

G. S. Sachdeva

Dr. G. S. Sachdeva has been one of the pioneer-scholars in India in the field of Space Law for three decades. He is Adjunct Professor, Centre for Air and Space Law, NALSAR University of Law, Hyderabad. He was formerly Adjunct Professor with the Centere for International Legal Studies, SIS, Jawaharlal Nehru University, New Delhi. He is also Guest Faculty at the West Bengal National University of Juridical Sciences, Kolkata and the Indian Academy of Diplomacy and International Law under the aegis of the Indian Society of International Law, New Delhi.

He obtained his Master's degree in Economics from the Delhi School of Economics, Delhi University and LLB, (Gold Medalist), from the Nagpur University. He pursued his research studies in International Law and was awarded the degrees of Master of Philosophy (M.Phil.) and Doctor of Philosophy (Ph.D.) from the Jawaharlal Nehru University, New Delhi. He completed his post-doctoral research at the Indian Society of International Law. He has written extensively in professional law journals and has edited books. He is the author of two books on space law, two books on air law and a monograph on space tourism.

He had served in the Indian Air Force (IAF) for 25 years and retired as a Wing Commander.

Deva Prasad M.

Mr. Deva Prasad M. is currently working as Assistant Professor of Law at the National Law School of India University, Bangalore. He has completed his undergraduate studies in law from the Gujarat National Law University and LLM from the National Law School of India University, Bangalore. He is also pursuing his doctoral studies in the international space law from the W.B. National University of Juridical Sciences, Kolkata. His areas of interest are international space law, environmental law and public international law. He has published articles on the international space law in reputed international and national journals including the *Acta Astronautica* and the *GNLU Journal of Law, Development and Politics*.

D. S. Govindrajan

Mr. Govindrajan is the President of Aniara Communications, where he is involved in the development of small GEO satellites and in creating business for the same.

Mr. Govind is an experienced satellite industry veteran with an experience in the sales, marketing and business development functions. He was Executive Director at Loral Orion and Loral Skynet from 1997 to 2006 where he headed sales and marketing for South Asia, Central Asia and East Africa. He was responsible for the introduction of satellite services for many new applications in the region. Prior to joining Loral, Mr. Govind worked with Hewlett Packard and for Forbes—an affiliate of the TATA conglomerate in India.

He has been a consultant for many leading organisations like Iridium Satellite, RaySatInc, Availink Inc. and has helped them to build their business in the region. As a widely travelled and well-known individual, he has nurtured an extensive network and personal rapport with the 'Who's Who' in the industry.

He is a Fellow of the IETE and an active member of various industry associations. He has an Engineering Degree in Electronics and Communications and a Master Degree in Management.

Ashok G.V.

Mr. Ashok G.V. is a practicing Advocate and Managing Partner, CorLit Legal.

He has represented start-ups, individuals and multinational enterprises in the litigations involving stakes in excess of Rs 450 crores (equivalent to USD 73 million) before the trial courts, the Hon'ble High Court of Karnataka, the Debts Recovery Tribunal, the Central Government Industrial Disputes Tribunal cum Labour Court and the Supreme Court of India.

Besides, Mr. Ashok has also devoted a significant number of hours in pro-bono cases. He has delivered a number of guest lectures and has a significant number of publications to his credit.

डॉ० जितेन्द्र सिंह

राज्य मंत्री (स्वतंत्र प्रभार),
उत्तर पूर्वी क्षेत्र विकास मंत्रालय ;
राज्य मंत्री, प्रधान मंत्री कार्यालय,
कार्मिक, लोक शिकायत एवं पेंशन मंत्रालय,
परमाणु ऊर्जा विभाग तथा अंतरिक्ष विभाग,
भारत सरकार

Dr. JITENDRA SINGH
Minister of State (Independent Charge),
Ministry of Development of North Eastern Region;
Minister of State, Prime Minister's Office,
सत्यमेव जयते Ministry of Personnel, Public Grievances and Pensions,
Department of Atomic Energy and Department of Space,
Government of India

New Delhi, dt. 16th July 2015

MESSAGE

'It gives me immense pleasure to note that National Law School of India University has taken an initiative in contributing to the foundation of Rule of Law in Outer space by organizing the Round table conference on 'Commercialization and privatization of Outer Space: Issues for National Space Legislation' on 18th July 2015. It may be a small step for the Law School but certainly a giant step towards defining our domestic legal regime for space activities.

I am aware that the National Law School of India University, Bangalore has been contributing to societal needs and has had a robust history in contributing to the law making process and I am pleased that this time as well the Law School, Bangalore is living to its name of providing insights for making laws for betterment of humanity. Given the robust space activities across the globe, it is indeed time that we open up discussions for a legal framework for commercial space activities.

Vigyan Bhavan Annexe,
Maulana Azad Road, New Delhi-110011
Tel. : 011-23022400, 23022401.
Fax. : 011-23062754

South Block, New Delhi-110011
Tel. : 011-23010191 Fax : 011-2307931
North Block, New Delhi-110001
Tel. : 011-23092475 Fax : 011-23092716

डॉ0 जितेन्द्र सिंह

राज्य मंत्री (स्वतंत्र प्रभार),
उत्तर पूर्वी क्षेत्र विकास मंत्रालय ;
राज्य मंत्री, प्रधान मंत्री कार्यालय,
कार्मिक, लोक शिकायत एवं पेंशन मंत्रालय,
परमाणु ऊर्जा विभाग तथा अंतरिक्ष विभाग,
भारत सरकार

Dr. JITENDRA SINGH
Minister of State (Independent Charge),
Ministry of Development of North Eastern Region;
Minister of State, Prime Minister's Office,
Ministry of Personnel, Public Grievances and Pensions,
Department of Atomic Energy and Department of Space,
Government of India

The significance of space activities for a developing nation like India was explained quite some time ago by Dr. Vikram Sarabhai. "There are some who question the relevance of space activities in a developing nation. To us, there is no ambiguity of purpose. We do not have the fantasy of competing with the economically advanced nations in the exploration of the moon or the planets or manned space-flights. But we are convinced that if we are to play a meaningful role nationally, and in the community of nations, we must be second to none in the application of advanced technologies to the real problems of man and society." Through space technology we have been catering the needs of society. The Village Resource Centre Programme, telemedicine, tele-education and many more have been exceptionally successful and this is only a beginning.

In the days to come we not only aspire to further develop space technology but also aspire to make space based solutions much more accessible to common man. Indeed, it is about time to acknowledge the significance of national space legislation and this round table conference is definitely a positive step taken by NLSIU in this direction.

I wish the conference all success.

16.7.15

(Dr. Jitendra Singh)
MBBS (Stanley, Chennai)
Medicine, Fellowship (AIIMS, NDL)
MNAMS Diabetes & Endocrinology

Vigyan Bhavan Annexe,
Maulana Azad Road, New Delhi-110011
Tel. : 011-23022400, 23022401.
Fax. : 011-23062754

South Block, New Delhi-110011
Tel. : 011-23010191 Fax : 011-2307931
North Block, New Delhi-110001
Tel. : 011-23092475 Fax : 011-23092716

Prologue

R. VENKATA RAO AND KUMAR ABHIJEET

With the advent of private players in the global space sector, commercial activity has been escalating. Today, private players have proven their technological and financial capacity and are doing wonders in space but with this great potential comes the greater responsibility. The responsibility is to ensure that space activities are safe; in compliance with India's international and Constitutional obligations, activities of non-governmental entities are 'authorized and supervised'. The time has come that India opens its door to outer space for private participants and promotes competition in the space market. A competition to promote space commerce; a competition to boost the nation's economy; a competition to resolve our societal problems.

This book is a compilation of the papers presented at the round table conference on "Commercialization and Privatization of Outer Space: Issues for National Space Legislation" held on July 18, 2015, organised by National Law School of India University (NLSIU), Bangalore in association with TMT Law Practice, New Delhi.

The conference was a platform for an interface between the academia, scientists, private space players, attorneys and various other stakeholders in outer space who can facilitate in defining the legal landscape for promoting the private space players. The book compiles the thoughts of the best of the academicians, space law attorneys and from the industry reflecting upon the commercial aspect of the space activities and the underlying legal landscape governing them.

All together, the book is a compilation of eleven articles, and four brief comments. The first among them is the "Potentials of Private Participation in Indian Space Sector: Policy And Legal Needs" written by Prof. K. R. Sridhara Murthi. His article highlights the two distinct segments of the 'Space Value Chain' of the Indian space sector—the first being ISRO as a dominant player of the Indian space sector and the other segment which is constituted by the industries in private and public sectors, which offer space-based commercial services in areas such as telecommunications, direct-to-home broadcasting, remote sensing data and information solutions and services including Geographic Information System (GIS) products/ services and manufacturing support as contractors to the national space agency's space projects. His assessment of the present Indian space sector is that (i) a robust policy and regulatory regime aimed at India's commercial space sector is the need of the hour. This regime has to address diverse goals and needs such as support for economic development, national and internal security, environment for innovations and investment, competitiveness and long-term sustainability, risk management and public–private partnership. (ii) It is necessary to assess real opportunities, risks and barriers, resources and capabilities for realising and sustaining such growth and diversification. (iii) Balanced roles of the government as well as the private sector are the realities that need to be integrated into the policy-making processes and structures.

In his article, he raises important issues: what are the key transforming factors that compel the need for growing and diversifying the role of the private sector in India's space activities? What are the short term and long term drivers? What specific avenues could be pursued to realise such an expanded role in future? He concludes that a National Space Policy and National Space Legislation are undeniable needs of the current times. The policy and legislations should foster a vibrant and equitable eco-system of government–private sector partnership and nurture systems that undertake an advanced technology development.

The second article is by Dr. G. S. Sachdeva on "State Responsibility for the Space Activities of Private Actors" He has elaborately explained the concept of State Responsibility and that of State Responsibility in space law. His concerns are regarding the increasing number of private actors in the space sector with no clarity in law in respect of regulating their conduct while at the same time, respective states are bound to bear the responsibility for their acts. He advocates that in order to properly acquit themselves of this responsibility, states may have to regulate and supervise private space activities by specific domestic legislation or modulation of national statutes to ensure that the space industry gets an impetus and causes least injury to a third party.

"National Space Legislation: What International Law Demands and How it is Implemented" written by Prof. (Dr.) Stephan Hobe focuses on the challenges for the space lawmaking and questions who are the actors, who are under an obligation to implement a space law for the private space activities. He has briefly sketched out the phases for space lawmaking and opines that the trend is towards less-binding "commitments". In the second part of his paper he has discussed the requirements for an international law concerning the private space activities. He suggests that any modern space power that considers the necessity for more private space activities is in the need of a national space law. A country like India that has already entered the arena of important space powers should therefore seriously consider having its own national space legislation. Otherwise, it risks being held liable for the activities of private entities whenever a link to India (territory, launching facility or the carrying out of a launch) can be established.

The fourth article written by Prof. (Dr.) V. Balakista Reddy is "Commercialisation of Remote Sensing and Geo-Spatial Data: Emerging Legal Jargons". His paper begins with a brief historical overview behind the development of the legal regime of remote sensing and thereafter familiarises with the UN Principles of Remote Sensing and conducts a discussion on its key provisions. The paper thereafter presents a critical review of the international space law regimes in governing remote-sensing activities with a special focus on the UN Remote Sensing Principles and finally examines critically the grey areas like the emergence of privacy rights, copyright infringement and concerns regarding the possible infringement of sovereignty. These issues have emerged with the technological development but till date are beyond the control and regulation of the international regime for remote sensing.

He expresses that Remote Sensing and GIS applications have become the focal point of the space technology and spacefaring nations are regularly using the same for both undisclosed and disclosed vested interests but unfortunately the legal regime existing under international space law for the governance of remote sensing and GIS Applications is in the form of a nonbinding set of ideals which the signatory nations are encouraged to abide by. His opinion is that the general international space law regime comprising of both the soft and hard law have become obsolete and is unable to match up with the technological development.

The fifth article "On Drafting A Viable Model of National Space Legislation for India" by Dr. Sandeepa Bhat B. reflects upon the various aspects of national space legislation. He discusses the licensing and supervision of the private space activities, the registration of launches, the liability for the damage caused and cautions regarding the emerging property rights in celestial bodies. Other issues which needs to be addressed are the prohibition of military activities, protection of the environment of outer space, the promotion of space tourism, patent protection in outer space, norms of private space financing and investment, dispute settlement and penalty provisions.

He is of the strong opinion that the drafting of a national space legislation has to be done by persons with a legal background and not by those with a scientific background because any failure to use the appropriate words would result in absurdity. He does not deny the need of assistance of the scientific community in drafting the legislation but utmost care should be taken in institutionalising the things. There is a narrow line of distinction between the interpretation and misinterpretation of laws. It is obvious that the miscreants would do their best to evade the law through misinterpretations and therefore, it is a challenge for the lawmakers to strengthen the four corners of law to overcome the problem of evasion. In the absence of such a crafty drafting, a law would be more of a menace than being of any use. He concludes that it is our duty to see that we are not setting a bad precedent in terms of space lawmaking.

Mr. Kumar Abhijeet writes on "State Practices Towards National Space Legilsation" reveling how various space faring nations have addressed the general issues of a national space legislation–scope and applicability, liability, authorisation, supervision, registration, indemnification, environment considerations, etc.

He expresses that there is no doubt that there is a lot to learn from the state practices towards the national space legislation but it must be kept in mind that the National Space Act of India should be drafted according to the Indian needs and requirement. The challenge in laying the draft lies in deciding the appropriate administrative authority for effective authorisation and supervision and a suitable dispute resolution mechanism. As the commercial exploration of space is going to increase in a magnificent manner with an increased participation from the private sector, a more specialised legislation shall be needed in the future depending upon the nature of the space activity.

The seventh article "Perspectives on Global Space Transport that may Begin Operations in Due Course" written by Prof. (Dr.) Saligram Bhatt was presented in absentia in the conference. He foresees the future of space transportation with private sector participation wherein is the necessity to provide regulatory environment. He outlines the major objectives and legal principles of space law that have similarity with the air law regime. He suggests the need of common board or governing body for the governance of space transport as space administration and aviation administration work in isolation.

Dr. Susmita Mohanty in her article "Manifesto for PSLV Privatisation" advocates for a privatisation of India's Polar Satellite Launch Vehicle (PSLV). She draws inspiration from the European, Japanese and American model and is of the opinion that the PSLV can successfully compete with the established and emerging launch providers if the Indian government liberalises the space economy. For this, the ISRO will have to accelerate its plans for the PSLV privatisation. She suggests the enactment of a Commercial Space Launch Act to encourage commercial space transportation systems and enable the Indian industry to build and operate the Expendable Launch Vehicles and Re-usable Launch Vehicles including future space planes for the space tourism industry. She recommends deregulation of the existing space governance, encourage privatisation and commercial use of space. At the same time, she also emphasises the creation of a safety and regulatory framework to enable a private access to space.

The ninth article "Space Law for Space Commerce or Vice Versa: A Chicken-and-Egg Situation for Space Commerce in India?" is written by Mr. Narayan Prasad. He views that due to a lack of deregulation and privatisation of India's space sector, currently there is no extensive commercial exploitation of the space infrastructure. Space commerce can be enabled by Public–Private Partnerships (PPPs), creation of business incubation centres/space parks for SME development, turnkey technology transfer programmes, creation of national funds for industry-led research in space, etc.; the governance aspect needs to address transparency in decision-making, avoidance of conflicts of interest, time-bound decision-making, focusing on the ease of enabling business, clarity in regulatory environment, etc.

He cautions that the National Space Legislation of India acts as an enabler for space commerce and not just to cover the international treaty obligations and suggests that the establishment of a comprehensive space legislation alongside the well-defined and transparent procedural aspects of commerce will promote a stable and predictable policy and regulatory environment that contributes to the success of the commercial space efforts, the entry of new entrepreneurs (including those not traditionally associated with the space activities), supports the private sector intellectual property and creates new market for space goods and services.

The tenth article "Policy Framework for Commercial Space Activities" is of Mr. Ashok G. V. His paper provides a snapshot of the broad range of topics that any policy for commercial space activities has to address. He is also sceptical with regard to space governance structure in light of the increased role of private space participants in future. He anticipates that to meaningfully encourage and enhance the private sector participation in India's space programmes, what is required is not just a single legislation but a broad range of legislative exercises including amendments to the many existing legislations.

The last article is by Mr. D. S. Govindrajan. In his paper tittled as "Commercialisation and Privatisation of Outer Space: Exploiting the Commercial Value of Space" he reflects upon achievements of Indian space programme and emphasises the emerging business opportunity and shift from the government to the commercial enterprises. He gives illustration of various space enterpreneurs and suggests India has to implement a proper policy and programme for the commercialisation of its space sector. The policy must provide lower barriers to entry which will attract more entrepreneurs enabling technological advancements and innovation, leading to new applications.

Four brief comments by Prof. (Dr.) Saligram Bhatt, "Space Law in the Age of Privatisation and Commercialisation"; Mr. Malaya Adhikari, "Institutionalisation of the Space Law in India"; Mr. Deva Prasad M., "The Private Space Activity Regulator's Role in the Space Environment Protection: A Policy Snapshot" and Mr. Prateep Basu, "Need for a Business Incubation in the Indian Space Programme", have also been included in this publication. Dr. Ranjana Kaul's summary paper—"National Space Law for India: Deconstructing the Proposition" has also been placed in the annexure.

The National Law School has always catered the societal needs and has had a robust history in the lawmaking process and this time also, the conference made an attempt for the betterment of laws. The meetings of the diverse, dynamic, enthusiastic, young and talented minds helped to draw the skeletal framework (see Annexure: Bangalore Declaration) of our intended legislation which may help the government concretise the draft bill in a better manner. The Bangalore Declaration is a beacon illuminating what a national space legislation should minimally address. In view of National Space Legislation of India being under the drafting process, it is believed that the book will be of significant practical value to all those interested in the rule of law in outer space.

The book addresses the various aspects of commercial space activity elucidates the necessity for a national space legislation, discusses the international obligation of India, reflects upon the relevant principles and rules of international space law; makes a study of laws of spacefaring nations, outlines the minimum legislative agenda as to what should be the content of such a legislation. It also discusses the legal issues relating to specific space activities like remote sensing, space transportation, privatisation of PSLV, etc.

The thoughts expressed in this book are the thoughts of respective authors and in no way reflect the thoughts of editors or National Law School of India University, Bangalore or the publishers.

Articles

1. Potentials of Private Participation in the Indian Space Sector: Policy and Legal Needs

K. R. SRIDHARA MURTHI

Global Space Economy and Private Sector

The Global Space Economy is characterised by a steady growth in value of commercial space activities, which now far exceed the budgetary allocations by governments on space activities. In 2014, the space economy grew globally more than 9 per cent as compared to the previous year, reaching a total of US$ 330 billion, according to a report by the US Space Foundation.[1] The Commercial Space activities constitute 76 per cent of the total space economy, while the rest are constituted by the public expenditures. The past two years have also seen a jump in the launch rate from an annual average of 105 satellites per year during 2000–2009 to 214 satellites in 2013 and 285 in 2014, the increase coming from a spurt of miniaturised (pico, nano and micro) satellites. In recent years, we have been witnessing a transformative growth in private sector's space activities, which have been encouraged and triggered by policy initiatives in several countries including the USA. An overall trend of reduction in government expenditures on space activities is also apparent. There have been disruptive innovations towards cost reduction, and an emerging scenario of 'New Space' initiatives by the private sector such as mission concepts involving large constellations of small or miniaturised spacecraft yet capable of high performance in delivery of information, communications and other services. These initiatives also address a host of new opportunities such as commercial cargo and crew transport, space tourism and affordable spaceflight, robots for lunar and planetary exploration and asteroid mining, expandable modules for space station and systems that address progress towards space colonies. In the context of such an emerging global environment, regulations are the key to a sustained development of commercial space activities and the private sector's increased role both at the national and international levels.

---

1. "The Space Report 2015: The Authoritative Guide to Global Space Activity". Space Foundation, Colorado Springs, CO 80907 USA.

India's Space Sector

India's accomplishments in space are remarkable. Yet, when it comes to commercial space activities, India has a long way to travel. Space activities in India over the decades had been driven by a strong role of the public sector. This was reinforced by the burgeoning societal needs that provided relevance for many a non-commercial application such as improved connectivity for rural populations, spread of literacy, improved forecasts of weather, disaster mitigation, sustainable use of natural resources, and so on. Rapid strides in the civilian space programme had been taken by India's Space Agency ISRO, which is organised directly under the Government of India, in achieving a self-reliant development of the state-of-the-art technologies for building, launching and manoeuvring spacecraft into a variety of orbits including lunar and Mars orbits, and their operations in space environment. A detailed appreciation of the accomplishments of Indian Space Programme over the years is dealt with in other references (Kasturirangan, 2014[2]) and hence not covered here. These span over 74 satellite missions and 47 launch missions executed by the national space agency with a comparatively high success rate and by setting some fine examples of international cooperation. What is noteworthy here is the availability of a total technology capability for the space systems in India and its still vast potential. The current annual budget for the civilian space agency constitutes 0.045 per cent of the national GDP, which is still modest but could grow further significantly in the context of a rapidly growing economy.

Two distinct segments of India's space sector are as follows.

- The government-funded space activities are largely executed by the national space agency, ISRO, which is under the Government of India. These include technology development, building space systems such as satellites and launch vehicles, their operations and development of a variety of applications and coordination among various government and non-government agencies for a wider use of space technology and systems. The agency also plays a pivotal role for developing/implementing policies, actively engages in the promotion of international cooperation, pursues scientific exploration in space, and has been enabling the societal development impacts from space technology applications. Although integrated into the Department of

---

2. "India In Space: A Conceptual Framework For The 21st Century", Dr. Satish C Seth Memorial Futurology Lecture series 5, delivered by Dr. K Kasturirangan, Indian Council of Management & Future, New Delhi.

Space of the Government of India, ISRO's legal personality is somewhat vague. De facto, it has manifested in a robust personality, influence and performance in terms of technical managerial capabilities and an ethos for holistic human development through space science and technology endeavours. ISRO is a dominant player in the Indian Space sector.

- The other segment of the Indian space sector is constituted by industries in the private and public sectors, which offer space-based commercial services in areas such as telecommunications, direct-to-home broadcasting, remote sensing data and information solutions and services including Geographic Information System (GIS) products/services and manufacturing support as contractors to the national space agency's space projects.

Both ISRO and the industry play a vital role in building and nurturing the 'Space Value Chain'. In the upstream elements of the value chain, apart from the domestic industry, the global industry has some significant share through supply/provision of high reliability electronic parts, materials, and capital equipment used in the manufacture and testing of space systems. The middle part of a value chain, consisting of space and ground infrastructure development (such as satellites, launch vehicles and so on) is shared by the space centres and units of ISRO and a large number of industrial enterprises of highly varying sizes both in the public and private sectors. It is significant to note that very few of them exclusively deal with space activities and most of them assume the role of contractors or subcontractors of space projects which are executed by the space agency. In the downstream part of the value chain, the private sector is active in providing remote-sensing applications and telecommunications-related services such as DTH and VSAT network applications under a competitive environment. An overall assessment of the present Indian space sector indicates the following status:

- The size of commercial markets directly dependant on the space systems is about four to five times in value as compared to the annual space expenditure of the government (which is equivalent to about 1 billion US dollars). However, linkage between the objectives of the government expenditures and the goals for the growth of commercial sector meeting national interests, priorities and opportunities is still somewhat tenuous. They are now in different silos, though there are some policies that take cognisance of entry barriers perceived by the private sector and permit the use of government owned space assets by the private sector. The main limitation of this system is that it is not proactive to the rapid creation and expandion of market opportunities. A robust policy and regulatory regime aimed at India's commercial space sector is the need of the hour. This regime has to address–no doubt–diverse goals and needs such as support for economic development, national and internal security, environment for innovations and investment, competitiveness and long term sustainability, risk management and public–private partnership.

- Further, the future expansion of the space sector is logically dependant on the growth and diversification of India's space industry. Otherwise, there will be an increasing reliance on imports. Therefore, the main need is to create an environment for growth and diversification of India's space industry. It is necessary in this context to assess the real opportunities, risks and barriers that affect such a development. Finally, it will be pertinent to examine the issues relating to the resources and capabilities for realising and sustaining such growth and diversification.

- Thirdly, giving a new turn to develop the space industry further requires an entry strategy. There are needs to orchestrate and harness the limited natural resources such as geostationary orbit slots and electromagnetic frequency spectrum and the availability of technological knowhow for the industry for the manufacture of space systems or their operations in space. The government should engage with the private industry, and indeed all stakeholders, in the policy development process. In the systems and processes followed for policy development in the past, there was a predominant accent of the government's role and use of space. This was logical for initial decades but the global environment has been changing. The dichotomies of competition and cooperation, and balanced roles of the government as well as the private sector, are the realities that need to be integrated into the policymaking processes and structures.

India's Private Sector Role: Future Potentials

A major question in the context of the foregoing discussion is: what are the key transforming factors that compel the need for growing and diversifying the private sector role in India's space activities? What are the short-term and long-term drivers? What specific avenues could be pursued to realise such an expanded role in the future? The response to these questions is briefly discussed here.

The key future market drivers for the Indian space sector have emerged from the transforming growth of India's economy. Several studies have reported that by 2030, India will be among the top three economies of the world. The major drivers that would create burgeoning demands for the space-based products and services are the decision support needs arising from the diverse needs and trends such as the urban shift of the population, the opportunities and demands offered by the demographic profile, huge needs of ICT-based services, requirements of education, health, mobility and environment sectors, robust demands for disaster warning and mitigation, national security, natural resources management and opportunities opening up through the continued globalisation trends. Some key indicators of demand drivers are presented in Figure 1. The implication of such a trend is that India has to gear up to launch and maintain over 200 satellites of operational class in the orbit within the next one to two decades. Forays are to be made in the new areas of exploration, development and use of space stations and the mining of space resources in the framework of an appropriate international cooperation.

The sectors in which space services and products are going to be demanded are illustrated in Figure 2. The demands on the commercial sector could arise from two distinct aspects, namely the domestic demands (India as a market) and overseas demands (India as a source of space systems and services in the global markets). This dual orientation in the Indian capabilities would offer wider scope and opportunities for the international collaborations and seek synergy. For the global and domestic companies, India will be a market for space-qualified parts, manufacturing and test equipment, launch services, space capacity leases, space insurance and mission support.

For international markets, the Indian contributions could be possible in the fields of satellites and satellite equipment/subsystems, launch services, leasing space segment capacity, remote sensing data and downlinks, ground equipment, software and mission support.

Without strengthening the industry capacity and capability and diversifying its roles through a process of engagement between the government and private sector, the aforementioned expansion of India's space sector is inconceivable. Several imperatives of space activities, such as dual use concerns and technology export regimes, long gestations and demands for large investments, higher risks and government budgetary constraints dictate the need for a mature government and industry cooperation and public–private partnerships. The extent of the involvement of the private sector will no doubt depend upon the market potential and the risks foreseen. Within the spectrum of possible commercial space activities, the extent of participation by the government or the private sector could vary depending on the nature of the individual branch of activity as illustrated in Figure 3.

Private Participation: Policy and Legal Needs in Different Segments
Global experience indicates that government policies had invariably had a major role in triggering investment and participation by the private sector in the field of outer space technologies and applications. It is also noteworthy to see that an avant-garde policy to attract the private sector participation and a conducive regulatory environment is indeed necessary but not the sufficient conditions. To provide long-term framework to those policies, it augurs well to formally adopt an overarching National Space Policy and make it widely transparent. It is also necessary that this is reinforced by a National Space Legislation. The relevant needs for policy renewals and legal developments are briefly touched upon in the following lines.

Space Launch Services
Indian launch vehicles are cost-effective and they can play a wider global role through commercial launch services. The ISRO through Antrix has been providing commercial space launch services from its well-proven PSLV and in the future it could also provide such services for heavier satellites through its GSLV launch vehicles. A further evolution of the expanded activities in the field of space launch vehicles including a significant increase in the launch rate would require a greater partnership with the industry involving (a) models for higher risk-sharing by the industry (b) the industry's transition to moving up higher in the value chain in the field of launch vehicle manufacturing (c) the strengthening of the consortium approach in manufacturing and the delivery of launch systems as well as a role in marketing.

Policy renewals are an urgent need in order to manage the risks of liabilities on the government. The principle of state responsibility in the International Space Law for activities by the private commercial enterprises and the likely liabilities on states providing launch services need special legal and policy measures to protect the interests of the governments against potentially huge claims for compensation. This would call for improving the authorisation procedures for commercial launches and for establishing a legal basis for the commercial launch services and their possible implications. For example, effective technology safeguard measures should be put be in place even as industry participation increases both in breadth and depth. Insurance for covering launch and in-orbit risks should be obligatory on the customers. Policies should clearly articulate the issues of launch safety obligations, the guidelines on procurement of launch services by the government, the use by the industry of ISRO's facilities, investment assistance for technology upgradation, implementation of national security guidelines, promotion of competitiveness and the policies on collaboration.

Remote Sensing and GI

India has built up a rich heritage in space-based remote sensing and its applications. In this segment, efforts are necessary to update the policies in order to reduce disharmony between the Indian and the global policies. A balance in the achievement of development goals and in the safeguarding of the national security interests will continue to be relevant. New advances in technologies including GIS tools have brought to the fore the need for legal developments for protecting privacy, addressing manifold issues of liability concerning GI and improving the mechanisms for regulation. A deeper study of the GIS policy perspectives was undertaken by the NIAS and published earlier.[3]

Satellite Communications Infrastructure and Services

A major need is to revitalise the implementation aspects of the SATCOM policy for establishing the Indian Satellite Systems in the private sector domain or through the public–private partnerships. The reasons for the private sector shying away from this area should be investigated with any lacunae needing an urgent redressal. In view of the needs for a multifold scaling-up in capacity, the development of large platforms and high throughput systems would need a greater attention. The policies for upscaling the manufacturing capacity commensurate with opportunities in the overseas as well as the domestic markets need to be considered. The coverage needs beyond the territory of India are also another area for policy initiatives. One of the key issues in this segment pertains to the facilitation of access to orbit/ spectrum for the private sector use and incentives for the industry to invest in space assets like communication satellites. It is also necessary to ensure the independence of the regulator's role and the removal of a conflict of interests.

3.   Mukund Rao and K. R. Sridhara Murthi, "Perspectives for a National GI Policy" (Report R 11 - 2012), National Institute of Advanced Studies, Bangalore, September, 2012. Report No: R11-2012. (www.nias.res.in/docs/R11-2012-GI-Policy.pdf).

National Space Policy and National Space Legislation

Although many fragmented policy initiatives have been taken in the past with regard to the various aspects of exploration and the use of outer space by India, the time has long been overdue for a comprehensive National Space Policy and National Space Legislation for India. The foremost aspect in this regard relates to Space Governance, which needs to be renewed and revitalised in the context of the newly envisaged space order for India and its potentially powerful role in the future global order. A comprehensive perspective of India's Space Governance in the light of future developments has been attempted in a recent publication by Kasturirangan.[4] The expanded mandate for outer space combining several important national and international dimensions, strong business and governance support functions, strategic security roles and exploration of possible future human destinations requires a review of the adequacy of the present structures including that of the Space Commission. The National Space Legislation needs to address several outstanding issues of the alignment needed between the international regulatory environment and the domestic laws. Specific legal provisions are necessary to deal with the questions of liability, which will become more pronounced with the growth of the private sector activities in space. Legislative initiatives regarding the insurance obligations of commercial payloads, registration, government authorisations and licensing, technology safeguards, Intellectual Property Rights and data protection, and measures to ensure competitiveness are also urgently required. In the international arena, India should help in shaping the future policies and legal norms keeping in mind their alignment to the national interests.

In conclusion, a National Space Policy and a National Space Legislation are undeniable needs of the current times. They should guide the long-term strategy of Indian Space with national capability building as a public goal. They should reflect a national commitment to provide operational space service in the country while promoting the Indian Space enterprise. The policy and legislations should foster a vibrant and equitable eco-system of government–private sector partnership and nurture the systems undertaking

---

4. K. Kasturirangan and K. R. Sridhar Murthy, "India's Governance in Outer Space: Past, Present and Future", *The Journal of Governance* (Jan 2015), IC Centre for Governance, New Delhi.

an advanced technology development.[5] As an enabler of future progress, the policy should catalyse the pioneering steps for human spaceflight and planetary exploration mission investments.

Figure 1. Long Term Demand Drivers for the Indian Space Sector

Driver	Current	2050	Demands on space
Economy	7.277 Tr $ (PPP) in 2014	GDP 86 Trillion$ (PPP) 1.3 bi. with income>120,000 INR	Public investment in space reaching modest 0.1% Of GDP or nearly 80 Billion USD (PPP)
Demography	1,31 bi in 2015 28% 14 years or below	Popul. 1.7 bi. Over 800 million working age between 2015-2035	Burgeoning demands on enterprenuership, thematic satellite constellations for health, education, agriculture etc
Natural Resources & Environment, Energy	Forest cover 69.79 mi ha. 200 GW Energy capacity	> 600 GW, clean energy Need 10% more water (1320 bi cu m) & clean access , Emission cuts	Space information support for green development
Knowledge and information needs	School education focus Higher education access issues Infrastructure gaps	Skill development focus Wideband connectivity for all villages Meeting Spectrum needs	High throughput and high performance systems , Capacity increase by a hundered fold

Figure 2. Diversified Sectors of Space Services and Products

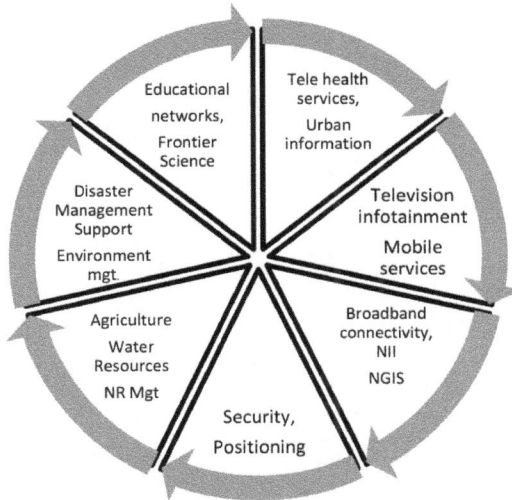

5. Dr. Mukund Kadursrinivas Rao, Prof. K. R. Sridhara Murthi and Dr. V. S. Ramamurthy,"Future Indian Space: Renewing Policy Dimensions", 65th International Astronautical Congress, Toronto, Canada, 2014.

Figure 3. Commercial Roles: Their Risk and Market Potential Profile

Canvas of Commercial Roles for India			
Market↓	**Private Sector**	**Private Sector+PPP**	**Public Sector Mainly**
Low Potential	Satellite systems	Space tourism, Crew modules, Cargo ferry	Human spaceflight, Space stations
Medium Potential	Small/ micro sats; Onboard equipment	Navigation equipment, hts satellites, launch vehicles	robots, rovers, landers, planet exploration
High Potential	Satellite services; contract manufacture	Broadband, High Res imaging, Location-based services	Space systems for national security
Risk levels and gestation→	Lower	Moderate	Higher

2. State Responsibility for the Space Activities of Private Actors

G. S. SACHDEVA

Introduction

It is axiomatic in international law "that state as a sovereign person, can have no legal responsibility whatever."[1] One graffiti says that the king can do no wrong. But such an absolute statement of classical law is no longer tenable in modern times and the contemporary law of nations admits a wider international liability for harm caused due to acts of State or certain internationally injurious acts committed by its agents, officials or nationals so authorised, enabled or ordered.[2] A correlative of this is the international duty cast by international pacts, treaties and conventions and out of these arise the *vinculum juris*—legal obligation to act within the confines of law and to assume responsibility for unauthorised injuries and violation of the international legal duty. It thus "is necessary to distinguish two different kinds of state responsibility. These may be named 'original' in contradistinction to 'vicarious' responsibility."[3] The original responsibility may comprise of international delinquencies and acts of state organs while the vicarious responsibility may relate to the acts of private persons who are nationals of the state.[4]

This tenet of state responsibility for its own acts, or of government functionaries or official organisations or its nationals, that cause international injury or damage, is a well-established principle of customary International Law. This has been embodied in the Space Law that is *lex specialis* for the outer space domain —so unique, hazardous and vulnerable. Till recently, the space activities which bear a long gestation period, involve highly complex technologies and require huge outlays with endemic risks of failure, were being undertaken by state agencies funded from the state exchequer. This trend of space exploration, however, is fast changing. Commercial space activities undertaken by private players, with no dependence on public funds, are the emerging trend.

1. L Oppenheim, *International Law A Treatise*, Vol. I, Peace, Seventh Edition, H. Lauterpacht (ed.), London, Longmans, Green & Co. (1952), 304.
2. Ibid., p. 306.
3. Ibid., pp. 305-7.
4. Ibid., pp. 304-34.

Indeed, it appears that the commercialisation of outer space is just round the corner. Space tourism has already caught the fancy of global tourists and safe technologies are under proof testing. Similarly, natural resources of the celestial bodies seem precious and utilisable on earth for the welfare of humanity. At the same time with advancing space technologies, their exploitation is becoming economically viable. Private enterprise has woken up to this prospective business potentiality and has embarked upon a profitability assessment. Remote sensing is another promising field. Space activity has, therefore, become a multi-billion dollar business segment with prospects of exponential growth.

Private enterprise in the form of public-private partnerships and individual ventures by billionaires and corporate conglomerates is gradually filling the widening hiatus created by the withdrawal of state patronage. These are the private actors in space activities in respect of whose conduct there is no clarity in law, but all the same, respective states are bound to bear the responsibility for their acts. In order to properly acquit themselves of this responsibility, the State may have to regulate and supervise their activities by specific domestic legislation or modulation of national statutes to ensure that the space industry gets impetus and still causes least injury to a third party or infringement of the space law resulting in a consequential international liability.

State Responsibility under the International Law

The principle of state responsibility is a classical doctrine of international law and has been adhered to for centuries almost as *jus cogens*; only new connotations of state responsibility have gradually evolved with the progressive times and the changing international milieu.[5] State responsibility is a correlative of international obligation and this concept constitutes the 'customary' legal mandate of a higher normative value. States as subjects of international law are bound by its tenets and are obligated to compliance with it .[6] This doctrine is thus expected "to serve as a specific instrument of legal regulation in international relations and stimulate the functioning of international law."[7]

---

5. The new concepts of state responsibility relate to, for example, war and aggression, coercion of minorities, denial of freedom by colonial powers, human rights violations and now extend to international and intergovernmental organisations.
6. Schwarzenberger, *International Law, Vol. I*, (3rd ed., 1957) , pp. 68-70.
7. Tunkin, G. I., *International Law*, Progress Publishers, Moscow, English translation, 1986, p. 223.

Many scholars of international law while discussing the substantive rules of rights and duties of the State assume that there exists a minimum international standard of justice and have highlighted the international responsibility of the States for breaches of duty, even by governmental authorities.[8] The scholars further assert that an international wrong committed by its nationals also "engages the responsibility of the State."[9] On the contrary, the State also has a bounden duty to ensure the safety and protection of its nationals and their assets in foreign countries in every possible manner whether legally, diplomatically or by alternative dispute-redressal methods.[10] Hence, ultra-hazardous activities like space activities should need a separate legal regime.[11]

In general terms, state responsibility pertains to the legal consequences of delinquent action of its legal entities, juridical persons and nationals that are now also treated as subjects of international law. In other words, responsibility attaches to the State upon the violation or a *delictum* as an act of commission or omission relating to any international legal obligation.[12] It may be added for clarity that the state responsibility extends to harmful consequences of even legitimate activities. Thus any failure or detrimental effect of an act, in turn, sets up a legal liability *qua* the aggrieved party of another State, subject to the basic rule that all means of domestic protection must first be exhausted. It seems pertinent to mention, in defence, that in theory and practice of international law, certain circumstances and specific situations exonerate or preclude state responsibility. Some examples are, use of force in self-defence, *force majeure* and national disasters.

There is another relevant aspect of state responsibility that can be sublimated to *ergaomnes* and this rule has since been recognised in customary international law that *paripassu* becomes applicable to the contemporary space law. The legal force of this particular obligation that is owed by the states to the international community as a whole has been identified and obliquely

---

8. Charles G. Fenwick, *International Law*, Bombay, Vakil, Feffer and Simons Private Ltd (1967), p. 333.
9. Ibid, p. 334. Also refer to Eagleton and Freeman cited in footnotes on the same page.
10. Michael Akehurst, *A Modern Introduction to International Law*, London, George Allen and Unwin (1980), pp. 88-102.
11. C. W. Jenks, "Liability for Ultra-Hazardous Activities in international Law", 117 *Recueil des Cours*, 99, p. 165 (1966). Also refer to John Kelsen, "State Responsibility for Abnormally Dangerous Activities", 13, HARV. INTL. L. J. 197, 238 (1972).
12. Schwarzenberger terms it "the effectivity of international law" and does not deem it to be of binding nature. Refer n. 10 *supra*.

highlighted by the International Court of Justice in the Barcelona Traction case,[13] among others. As a result, this humanitarian duty of the state towards the humanity at large has been accepted universally and has got deeply rooted in state practice. In fact, state responsibility *ergaomnes* has been elevated to the status of *jus cogens* of space law[14] and can consequently draw substantive support from the Vienna Convention.[15] Such a responsibility would be equally incumbent on the private actors during space activities.

Yet another aspect of state responsibility stems from the national constitutions and domestic statutes. For example, the Indian Constitution directs under Article 51 "to promote international peace and security" as well as "foster respect for international law and treaty obligations…" Indeed, the language of the Directive is clear and explicit. And, Article 253 of the Constitution empowers the Parliament to make suitable and appropriate laws to implement the provisions and obligations under any treaty, agreement or convention ratified by the State.

State Responsibility under Space Law

The necessity of a space law arose to regulate the human activity in outer space and the operation of human-made objects in that domain. Thus, the primary purpose of law is to ensure peace and order by informing normative behaviour and regulating human activity. A Spanish proverb succinctly sums up this wisdom and it states that it is not the fence that protects the orchard, but the fear that goes with it and this element of fear, to a certain extent, is imparted and instilled by the law to substantially achieve its purpose and consequently security and public order seem assured.

By corollary, this principle can be safely extended to outer space where this *lex specialis* performs a vital function by its proclamations of permitted, prohibited and regulated activities. Space law thus defines the nature of activities in outer space and stipulates the norms of human conduct in relation to this medium. Hence, this law seems to promote public order in outer space. This specific law that is mostly comprised of a few treaties, agreements and soft law formulations of principles and declarations has, by and large, succeeded in achieving this task within the outer space.

---

13. Barcelona Traction, Light and Power Co. *(Belgium v. Spain)* 1970 ICJ 3, 32 (5 February, 1970).

14. For a detailed analysis on *Jus Cogens* of Space Law, refer G. S. Sachdeva, *Outer Space: Law, Policy and Governance,* New Delhi, KW Publishers (2014) 1-30.

15. *The Vienna Convention of the Law of Treaties*, 1969, Article 53. Articles 27 and 46 are also relevant.

To mention in passing, the space law grew as an adjunct of International Law and has metabolised rather fast. It is now getting metamorphosed into an independent and auto-poietic system[16] with complexities and cross-linkages with other subsystems of cognate legal regimes,[17] international jurisprudence, objects and subjects of law, their operations and applications. It has, in turn, imbibed a fairly evolved concept of state responsibility which has been enshrined in the Outer Space Treaty (OST)[18] as well as other international instruments of space law.

State Responsibility under the Outer Space Treaty

The principle of state responsibility echoes in the OST from several aspects and at several planes. First, Article III of the OST stipulates that "State parties to the treaty shall carry on activities in the exploration and use of outer space, including the Moon and other celestial bodies, in accordance with international law, including the Charter of the United Nations..." This implies that the concept of state responsibility as developed in international law shall become part of space law and equally applicable to space activities. Secondly, Article VI of OST provides a direct nexus between state responsibility and national activities in outer space. It states, "State parties to the Treaty shall bear international responsibility for national activities in outer space, including the Moon and other celestial bodies." This provision is obligatory and binding.

Thirdly, under the umbrella of responsibility, Article VII of the OST highlights an associated aspect of international liability for third-party damage. The clause reads, "Each state party to the Treaty that launches or procures the launching of an object into outer space, including the Moon and other celestial bodies, and each state party from whose territory or facility an object is launched, is internationally liable for damage to another state party...or to its natural and juridical persons...on the Earth, in air space or in outer space, including the Moon and other celestial bodies." Its plain reading seems to cause confusion as a rather undefined liability that is attached to multiple parties. The concerned parties may, however, have an internal back-to-back agreement on contracting out of liability, sharing of liability or seek indemnity for such obligation.

---

16. Anthony D'Amato, "International Law as an Autopoietic System" in Rudiger Wolfrum and Volker Robens, (eds,) *Developments of International Law in Treaty Making,* Springer, Berlin, 2005, pp. 335-399.
17. For example, regimes for Global Commons like Antarctica, High Seas, etc.
18. Treaty on Principles Governing the Activities of States in the Exploration and Use of Outer Space including the Moon and other Celestial Bodies, 1967.

State Responsibility under Other International Instruments

The fundamental of state responsibility finds a portfolio of copious references scattered in other international instruments regulating space activities either as a direct reference or by its generic variants like the duty to assist in emergencies and distress or offer cooperation or engage in consultations for unusual events and potentially dangerous experiments, etc. A few examples can be adduced to vindicate the above statement.

The Convention on International Liability for Damage Caused by Space Objects, 1972 amplifies the provision of responsibility and liability, skeletally mentioned in the Articles VI and VII of the OST, and outlines the procedure for incumbent claims. The Moon Agreement[19] too carries a definitive and specific clause on this point. It states, "States party to this Agreement shall bear international responsibility for national activities on the Moon, whether such activities are carried on by governmental agencies or by non-governmental entities…" And states shall assure that "national activities are carried out in conformity with provisions set forth in this Agreement."[20] This call for an adherence to the law is loud and clear.

Modes of Management of Space Activities

There can be different modes of managing the space activities. Considering its peculiarities, two factors rise in sharp focus: technological competence to operate in outer space and the financial model that determines the business organisation. The former assumes importance because space technology is an integrated and composite group of sub-technologies like launch rocket, fuel optimisation, satellite fabrication, systems jointing, tracking on earth, mission direction and so on. This wide spectrum of technologies is not easy for the private actors to effectively muster under one control centre, which makes it prone to state-centric suitability for ownership and operability. Further, space technology needs continuous research, modifications over a wide range of hardware and a constant updation of operational nuances.

The second aspect of financial funding governs the management model. It is undeniable that the activities capable of operation in outer space require a huge funding not only for mission performance but also for research and failure remediation. The resultant capital outlays and operational costs can run into billions of dollars which invite different patterns of investment.

---

19. Agreement Governing the Activities of States on the Moon and Other Celestial Bodies, 1979, popularly referred to as the Moon Agreement.
20. Ibid., Article 14.

First, state ownership gets public funding from the exchequer and is almost limitless based on budgetary demands. In a variation from this, there can be government-driven investment with speed or equity contribution and the rest coming from other public sector or private organisations.

Apart from the above, total investment can also emerge from the private sector as venture capital or pure corporate finance. In fact, many corporate conglomerates (like Mitsubishi, Boeing Defense) and individual entrepreneurs (like Richard Branson, Elon Musk) have entered the business and are operating rather successfully, too. Many start-up companies are waiting in the wings. It will be of particular interest as to how the established space companies can strategically position themselves with regard to the new fledgling competitors.

State Agencies

Historically, for the last half a century, in most countries, government departments have managed space activities through state-funded, state-controlled, state-managed, closed-door agencies and research centres that have worked on state directives for overt and covert objectives, mostly in utter disregard for principles of economics or canons of audit. The orientation here was state-centric and authoritarian with a sole focus on public interest and devotion to strategic concerns. Of course, research activities are a unique domain and move at their own pace, usually in fits and starts. But the proof of research lies in success and some countries have achieved remarkable results with laurels. India is a fitting example of such a scenario.

Another mode of space activities permitted in the OST pertains to joint operations with state parties or other states that are non-adherents to the OST.[21] Here again, activities are usually performed by the public sector undertakings in a state-centric domain. The Treaty drafters, it seems, had visualised possibilities of joint efforts in space ventures, like procurement of launches or satellite operation, with other states that are either or not, party to the OST. The germane provision stipulates, "Treaty shall apply to the activities of states parties...in the exploration and use of outer space, including the Moon and other celestial bodies, whether such activities are carried on by a single state party...or jointly with other states, including cases where they are carried on within the framework of international intergovernmental organization."[22] This again is a mode of the state-centric management of affairs.

---

21. n. 19, supra, Article XIII.
22. Ibid.

Private Actors

Till a decade ago, space activities were undertaken by state organisations with total allegiance to the national objectives. This was because space activities involve arduous research, long gestation period to fruition, coordination of highly complex technologies and huge outlays in projects beset with uncertainties. Meanwhile, actual operations involve several international implications. No wonder, such activities were undertaken by state agencies funded from the state exchequer. This trend of scientific exploration and military advancement is today significantly shifting to commercial avenues with an emphasis on business parameters. Thus, the rationale and justification for state funding is weakening for the developed countries like the US, and space activities, except for strategic imperatives, are progressively being weaned off from public funds.[23] This trend will soon find ground in other countries also.

Therefore, commercial uses of outer space and the exploitation of natural resources of celestial bodies are in the offing. New entrepreneurs are rushing into the space business race. Space tourism is already becoming fanciful and fashionable for elites. Similarly, the natural resources of celestial bodies, including asteroids, seem precious and utilisable on earth for better lifestyles of living. At the same time, with advancing space technologies and increasing automation, their exploitation is becoming economically viable and operationally simpler. Private enterprise has woken up to this prospective reality of business potentialities and has embarked on a serious assessment of feasibility in technology, viability of operations, market response, magnitude of investment funding and economics of returns.

Even space manufacturing and celestial industrialisation have animated human imagination and currently experiments and pilot projects in sterile and gravity-free environment of outer space are being undertaken. These relate to the manufacture of vaccines and high quality crystals, to name just a few. Space activity, therefore, if things go according to plan, is poised for a big surge to become a multibillion dollar business segment with prospects of exponential growth. Private enterprise in the form of individual ventures by billionaires and corporate conglomerates is gradually filling the widening hiatus created by the withdrawal of state activities, especially in the USA. We may thus be entering an era of 'New Space Economics' with private actors.

---

23. Also refer A Latipulhayat, "Privitization of Space Law: Negotiating of Commercial Benefit-Sharing Issues in the Utilization of Outer Space" in Corine Jorgenson, ed. *Proceedings of IISL, 2012* (The Hague, Eleven International Publishing, 2013) 247.

These are the private actors in space activities in respect of whose conduct the respective states shall bear responsibility. In fact, aggressive initiatives of the corporate community became apparent and irresistible during the UNISPACE-III conferences in 1999 and their future role in space activities was well recognised and their coexistence with the state agencies was accepted, though as a tacit and unwritten understanding. This trend has since become more pronounced as NASA has started using this route for cargo replenishments and crew transportation to the International Space Station (ISS). Nevertheless, some anomalies were discernible in the corpus of space law and the juridical identity of the private actors and their mandatory regulation and supervision was left to be complemented by state laws.

Generally, private actors can be of three types. First, public sector undertakings that could be outsourced with systems or subsystems which are subsequently integrated in space objects. Secondly, joint ventures on the public–private partnership model, with or without technology transfer, are the ones that could participate more actively in the fabrication of space objects or the launch vehicles. Thirdly, exclusive private corporations that could cooperate with a space agency or operate entirely independently in space activities like Virgin Galactic or Boeing Defense or SpaceX or Mitsubishi. Examples can be multiplied even though the nature and character or participation of the private actors may differ in different countries. But all the same, their business objective is good revenue, assured with a decent longevity and a break-even point of profit in the shortest time.

Private Actors in India

The situation in India is quite different from that of the US or Japan. Here, in a state-centric policy, ISRO retains monopoly of planning and production for space projects while privatisation exists at different tiers of technology, mostly of subsystems. Most of the private actors possess limited potential and a relatively low-end technology and generally constitute a second line of support through the indigenisation of non-critical supplies. In spite of limitations, they are striving to seek a transfer of technology from the ISRO, incrementally in bits and pieces, and aspire to grow big one day and hopefully turn India into an industrial space power.[24]

There is another set of bigger corporate houses that are making responsive gestures to the ISRO for collaboration and many of them have a

24. Aaron Chase, *India: An Investor's Guide to the Next Economic Superpower* (Singapore, John Wiley & Sons, 2006) p.8ff.

past association of cooperative partnership and have delivered commendable aerospace business. A few firms in this category are bulleted below:

- Walchandnagar Industries Ltd, Pune
- Larsen and Toubro, Mumbai
- Bharat Heavy Plates and Vessels Ltd, Vishakhapatnam
- International Marketing and Services, Bengaluru
- Tata Advanced Materials Ltd, Bengaluru
- Vantage Technologies, Chandigarh
- Komoline Aerospace Ltd, Ahmedabad
- Accord Software and Systems (P) Ltd, Bengaluru
- BrahMos Aerospace Ltd, Thiruvananthapuram
- Godrej and Boyce Manufacturing Co. Ltd, Mumbai

Apart from above, there are about 500 small and medium licensee companies which have received a technology transfer from the ISRO for commercial production and even a public marketing of products since many of these have applications in non-space sectors.[25] The Department of Space has transferred 290 technologies to the Indian industry and the transfer process is still in progress despite hassles of patents and intellectual property rights. Nonetheless, the modalities of the transfer procedure need to be institutionalised and made more transparent to seek the optimal support from a willing industry.[26] Besides the domestic companies, several foreign big corporate names are also keen on a cooperative participation with ISRO. To name a few, the Airbus Defense and Space has a centre at Bengaluru and the Thales Alenia Group as specialists in satellite manufacturing has a branch office; so has the Virgin Group shown its presence in the country because India appears to be a sleeping business giant.[27]

Analysis of the Permissibility of Private Actors
There is no direct and explicit provision in the OST or in any international instrument on space law or the UN Guidelines and Principles regulating space activities that clearly permits the private corporate sector to independently engage in space activities. This appears to be the silence of the times

25. Information available on the ISRO website.
26. More details on the topic available in Malay Adhikari, *International Legal Regulation of Private Actors in Outer Space: A Study of India's Role* (Jawaharlal Nehru University, 2015, unpublished Doctoral Thesis).
27. Ibid.

because when the OST was being negotiated, the possibility of private actors commercially entering the space domain with independent space activities was unthinkable and hazily envisioned. Today, of course, this presents a legal dilemma which can be resolved by juridical inferences or a liberal interpretation or by a logical vindication of the existing provisions of law.

Let's first draw strength from the *traveaux preparatoires* of the OST. The record of discussion on the negotiations indicates that the Soviet group advocated space activities to be an exclusive domain of the governmental space agencies to the exclusion of all other business segments. On the other hand, the US was keenly interested in relaxing and extending the provision of the Treaty to non-governmental organisations and other shades of private entities.[28] Thus, protracted negotiations gave a new meaning and connotation to the "national activities in outer space" and the very complexion of the Article VI of the OST changed. The US vision of the future stakeholders in space activities has turned out to be more realistic.

Article VI of the OST thus turns out to be highly relevant and equally pertinent. Its text reads, "States Parties to the Treaty shall bear international responsibility for national activities in outer space, including the Moon and other celestial bodies, whether such activities are carried on by governmental agencies or by non-governmental entities…" Here 'non-governmental entities' are not defined or the scope restricted. A reasonable jurisprudential construction of this term can comfortably include the corporate sector, private actors and individual entrepreneurs. But the rider of the state responsibility for national activities becomes highly significant and assumes importance.

To support in tandem, the above provision also echoes in the Moon Agreement and requires an assurance "that national activities are carried out in conformity with the provisions set forth in this Agreement."[29] This obligates compliance on all national activities in outer space irrespective of the performing entity. Further, Article III of the OST superimposes another conscious condition that the activities in outer space and on celestial bodies shall be in accordance with international law (and the Charter of the United Nations). And under its contemporary version, individuals as well as

---

28. Bin Cheng, Article VI of the 1967 Space Treaty Revisited: 'International Responsibility', 'National Activities' and 'The Appropriate State'", *Journal of Space Law*, 26(1), (1998) 14. Malay Adhikari, *International Legal Regulation of Private Actors in Outer Space: A Study of India's Role* (JNU, Doctoral Thesis, 2015, unpublished) 57.

29. n. 20, Article 14.

corporate organisations are deemed as subjects of the modern international law.[30]

There is, however, another rider clause under Article VI that mandates that "The activities of non-governmental entities in outer space, including the Moon and other celestial bodies, shall require authorization and continuing supervision by the appropriate State Party to the Treaty." The use of word 'shall' makes this requirement binding for a proper discharge of the international responsibility by the state, whosoever is the performer of space activity. The above provision of the OST finds almost a *verbatim* reiteration in the Moon Agreement.[31]

The above-mentioned provisions amply support the contention that private actors, in contradistinction to state agencies, can engage in space activities as independent players and stakeholders, subject to the following conditions:

- That activities in the outer space and on celestial bodies shall be in consonance with the provisions of the Treaty (Article VI of the OST).
- That activities shall be in accordance with international law, including the Charter of the United Nations (Article III of the OST).
- That the state party shall bear international responsibility for national activities in outer space including the Moon and other celestial bodies (Article VI of the OST).
- That each state party that launches or procures the launching of or from whose territory or facility an object is launched into outer space or to a celestial body is internationally liable for any damage to another state party (Article VII of the OST).
- That the state party shall ensure a proper authorisation and continuing supervision of the space activities by non-governmental entities (Article VI of the OST).
- That the state party shall ensure that the launching made or procured by the private actors is reported to the state registry and in turn communicated to the UN Office of Outer Space Affairs.[32]

Governance of Private Actors

In deference to the mandate of the OST, it becomes incumbent on the

---

30. Modern International Law includes the International Trade Law. There is, however, a divergence of views among the scholars and some treat these entities as 'objects'. Refer n.7 supra, p. 147ff.
31. n. 20 supra, Article 14.
32. Convention on Registration of Objects Launched into Outer Space, 1975.

states to regulate, monitor and continuously supervise the national space activities undertaken by the nongovernmental organisations including the private actors. The state governance must make sure that the space activities undertaken by its nationals are carried out as per the provisions of the relevant international law as well as being in concordance with the various treaty stipulations. Another important aspect is that the governance should be minimal and not restrictive or obstructive. On the contrary, it should be facilitative and conducive to the promotion of healthy business competition and technological innovation. The governance should be of three types— legal, normative and institutional.

Legal through Lex Specialis

India as a spacefaring nation is a state-party to almost all the international Space Treaties and Agreements and has as such, legal obligations to discharge and assure compliances for its activities in outer space and that of its nationals under the doctrine of state responsibility. India has, so far, been unfailingly complying with such obligations *qua* other states and the international community. Additionally, Article 51 of the Constitution of India places a solemn obligation on the state to promote international peace and security, including the maintenance of just and honourable relations between nations and a respect for international law and treaty obligations. India, of course, is a good example of model international behaviour but the compliance to international obligations is not dependent or contingent upon national laws nor can the lack of domestic statutes can be a reason or excuse for dereliction.

Besides this, space activities impinge on many other areas of national concerns that are regulated by legislation of either the Central or State government or by both under the Concurrent List in the Constitution. To illustrate, a few examples are foreign affairs, armed forces, trade and commerce, local taxes, labour laws, space insurance, etc. Differences are thus endemic in the system and a constitutional impasse can possibly occur. Thus, the existing informal legal framework and organisational structure is grossly inadequate for the prospective demands and future potential of the space industry in India. Therefore, a specialised legal framework (*lex specialis*) seems imperative in order to provide a due impetus to the pace of the rapidly growing and multi-dimensional space activities. This has to be effectively coupled with an enhanced participation of the private industry and to fully exploit the versatility of the ever-advancing space systems and their applications in the national interest and for international exports.

However, a caveat is that the law must be competent and yet encourage new belief systems.

Of course, by a liberal interpretation, inferential references and legal activism, private players are, today, deemed to be legitimate operators in the outer space for lawful activities under proper regulation and continuous supervision of the state. At the same time, the state has constitutional obligations as well as duties under the germane domestic laws that permit of no infringements of international law. And, on the international plane also, there exists state responsibility, international liability and an obligation towards the compliance of international treaties and conventions. Cumulated, it makes an onerous responsibility which cannot be fully discharged by sheer administrative directives, waiver contracts, indemnity agreements and other business modalities. Therefore, a specialised law remains of essence in the business beyond earth.

Further, commensurate with the exponential growth of technologies in the field of space-based systems for exploration and their applications in the global context, the Indian space segment seeks to sustain and maintain a leadership role in its niche space activities through appropriate programmatic plans and policy guidelines. This focuses on the necessity for a Space Act, with the aim and object to steer, promote and regulate the space activities in India for the overall national development purposes including national security[33] in all its phases—namely, cogitation, initiation, experimentation, development, proto-types, fabrication, integration, operational, commercial and expansionist. The law, therefore, must remain an enabling instrument to encourage technological innovation and to promote an optimal competition in space products and services.

This highlights the necessity for an umbrella domestic legislation which provides for a specialised governance in two prongs. One may address the domestic issues of licensing, regulation of manufacture, possession and export of space products and services, execution of space activities and compliance of stipulations. The other prong of the national law could relate to an adherence to international treaty obligations, modalities for the sharing of international liability for damage or injury in outer space, supervision of activities of private actors and arrangements for a possible help to them in distress and emergencies.

Legal controls could also cover aspects of security and confidentiality of space activities, on the ground and in outer space, so as not to jeopardise

---

33. Such an Act is under drafting by the ISRO.

vital state interests or to divulge covert intent. The other important aspect concerns the primacy of launch safety and mission success. This requires the highest standards of quality assurance in production to sustain a zero-failure tolerance or six-sigma quality resulting in the highest success rate. The national law may stipulate suitable checks for quality control and inspection of compliances to achieve these avowed aims in space activities.

New Ethics for Space Commerce—Through a Normative Lens

Any law, howsoever stern in content, is generally susceptible to loopholes through which the business operators can get past legally and indulge in activities that are not so lawful. Such chinks can be plugged by soft law. Therefore, apart from legal controls, there is need for an evolved economic mindset for space business and commercial engagements in outer space. With a high influx of space business round the corner, we should imbibe new ethics for space commerce. This seems all the more important because human beings, in their economic history on the Earth, have not acquitted themselves with glory and have indulged in slavery, colonial exploitation, iniquitous returns, conflictive management–labour relations, greed for entrepreneurial profit, berated trade practices, cartels and monopolies—to name just a few. Even the business philosophy of contemporary economics in maximisation of returns is not too laudable while its own assumptions of 'rationality of man' and 'returns on factors of production' are in turmoil. The remedy lies in higher business values, ethical trade practices and the commercial morality of a superior order.

Hence, on the verge of space commercialisation, let's not carry a dispensable baggage of such condemned practices, baser values and fixed mindset. We should attempt to evolve new space ethics that are more oriented towards a common good than individual returns; business houses may exhibit a due regard to corporate social responsibility (CSR), devote a conscious effort towards the sustainability of the space environment and develop a commitment to the humane treatment of the labour working in lonely, inhospitable and hazardous conditions of outer space or celestial bodies or space laboratories. The new business ethics should be imbued with law and justice, equity and fair play and a legitimacy of valid interests.

It is submitted that the United Nations may initiate action to propagate such a thought process through the Committee on Peaceful Uses of Outer Space (COPUOS) to enunciate and codify the Normative Guidelines for a new culture of cooperation and assistance in space and for a business based on moral values, ethics of commercial conduct and trade discipline for economic ventures in outer space and on celestial bodies, whether undertaken by the government organisations, joint ventures of states, entities of public–private partnership, corporate enterprise or through private individual endeavours.[34]

Appropriate Institutional Framework

In any organised activity, there has to be an in institutional axis around which the rights and duties of the partners in the activity and other stakeholders are to be balanced and harmonised. Further, since a conflict of interest is inevitable, sooner or later, a dispute redressal mechanism becomes necessary and even imperative for settlement–inducement, conflict resolution and for dispensing justice. These instrumentalities could be formal or informal depending upon the confidence of the parties in the competence of the system, nature of the settlement awards and mechanics of enforcement.

Based on the above postulate, the stakeholders can be identified as the state government, the entrepreneurial corporate and work force in the outer space. Of all three, the 'space worker' is the weakest party and in the most vulnerable situation. No wonder, his/her welfare needs protection from all angles through the intervening government assurances, contractual guarantees in the employment contract and a certain strength in his/her numbers—perhaps, through unity in fraternity. Basically, the safety of the space worker should assume primacy and his safe return to the earth, a sacrosanct vow. Though discipline and contractual compliance by the labour are cardinal duties, yet a benign unionised system may afford the workforce a bargaining strength and confidence to fight against occasional injustice; but, the reaction of the labour should never become disruptive or violent. In equity, you always go with clean hands.

Similarly, the comity of entrepreneurs too needs an association or a forum for an informal networking and discussion of common problems, a system for self-regulation and a representative body for the formal representations of grievances to the regulatory authority. It could be like the Chamber of Commerce which may also set the norms of business values and standards of healthy trade practices to infuse a new commercial mindset and belief system to approach the space activities. This is important because space is the gateway to the future of humankind. The proposed chamber

---

34. For more details on the topic, refer to "New Ethics for Space Commerce" in G. S. Sachdeva, *Outer Space: Security and Legal Challenges* (New Delhi, KW Publishers, 2010), pp. 105-126.

may also mediate in resolving minor issues and facilitate a settlement of disputes under the alternative redressal mechanisms. At the same time, the corporate world equally owes to, and is accountable to, the investors that it manages the space activities in the best interest of the space workers and discharges them with minimal conflict or liability. Profit cannot be the prime motivator in such a unique arena of business.

State responsibility is multidimensional in enforcing the rule of law i.e. accountability to the state legislatures, compliances in international domain and protection of its nationals and their assets in outer space and elsewhere. The sum total of state responsibility is indeed onerous and needs to have in place appropriate institutional support systems. Diplomatic channels can normally ensure protection and emergency assistance to nationals in distress while in outer space or on return. Compensation claims for liability can also be pursued with foreign law courts through consular help.

On the contrary, international liability incurred for infringement by any national space activity including those of private actors shall, in the first instance, fall on the state as per the provision of the Liability Convention, 1972. The nature of liability is absolute and the launching state cannot escape it.[35] Thereafter, it may be indemnified in any manner under a contractual arrangement or shared to be reimbursed by the delinquent private actor in part or in full or claimed from the insurance. Incidentally, compensation awarded against liability by any competent court is paid out of the Consolidated Fund of India, as per the Constitution and Rules of Business[36] framed thereunder.

Conclusion

Initially, space activities were state-sponsored, state-governed and state-funded because such activities represented an advancement of technology and offered strategic advantages. While these motivations still prevail, this sole reason has somewhat been eroded in its importance. Multimedia applications, possibility of space transportation and viability of commercial exploitation of celestial resources are becoming prospective business propositions. As a result, states are restricting investment to strategic research only and commercial ventures are passing on to private enterprise. And it is here that the private actors find their specific niche.

---

35. Convention on International Liability for Damage Caused by Space Objects, 1972, Article II.
36. Rules of Business carry the force of law as valid as a statute.

Space law has no explicit provision permitting activities of the private enterprise in outer space. Logical construction and legal inferences provide a window of opportunity. This view has, of course, come to be accepted by many scholars of international law. Further, the provisions relating to state responsibility and international liability are too generic to cover the different kinds of national activities in outer space. And, national activities can be undertaken by any national juridical entity or legal person as private actors. And, the grey areas in this scenario would become residual obligations of the state unless lawfully shared with the other stakeholders.

The above logic is certainly not fallacious. Yet, it carries a rider of state regulation and continuing supervision and compliance of the treaty law. This obligation necessitates a specialised domestic space statute, as an enabling tool, to ensure the adherence to treaty provisions and that there are no infringements of any sort by the actors in space activities and breaches, if any, would attract sanctions. Moreover, the incurrence of liability may also seem inevitable, however minimal, due to the highest standards of diligence and safety. Possible legal solutions and methods of redressal may also be contained in the national legislation.

On the domestic front, licensing procedures, scope of authorisation and supervisory practices should be clearly defined with the attendant consequences of infractions. Wisdom ordains a holistic space legislation that is comprehensive and proactive so as to provide a due fillip to the privatisation of space activities with optimal governance. Meanwhile, the private enterprise is expected to undertake its ventures in this sphere of global commons with a due respect for the fragility of the environment and the equity of the rights of others. Safe, secure and sustainable use of outer space has per force to be the collective responsibility of all the actors in this domain—State or private or their combinations. None can afford to be a weak link.

3. National Space Legislation: What the International Law Demands and How it is Implemented

STEPHAN HOBE

In the era of globalisation, space activities are undergoing a certain change. At the beginning of the space age in 1957, we had almost only public space activities, e.g. governments were sponsoring these activities. Today, i.e. 50 years later, there is an emerging private market for space activities. Take the launching sector: the United States of America has ceased its publicly sponsored "Space Shuttle"programme and rely solely on private launching. And other areas do it alike. Therefore, a new phase of international space law is necessary and about to start: a law of private space lawmaking. The current paper will deal with the challenges for the space lawmaking and will ask who are the actors, who is under an obligation to implement a space law for the private space activities and what form should these activities have.

Therefore in the following, I will briefly sketch out the phases for space lawmaking before the second section in which the requirements of international law concerning the private space activities will be described and in the third section examples will be given. Then the ILA Model Draft and the current activities of the United Nations Committee on the Peaceful Uses of Outer Space will be described before the final conclusion which will be given with regard to the possible activities of India.

The Phases of Space Lawmaking

There seems to be more and more unanimity in distinguishing space lawmaking into three different phases. The first phase, certainly driven by the publicly sponsored space activities, was the phase of hard lawmaking. Between 1957, the inception of the space age after the successful launch of the artificial satellite Sputnik I, and 1979, five international agreements were drafted and adopted: The Outer Space Treaty of 1967; the Rescue Convention of 1968; the Liability Convention of 1972; the Registration Convention of 1975 and finally the Moon Agreement of 1979. Yet, the number of ratifications for these conventions varies considerably. It ranges from 103 ratifications of the Outer Space Treaty of 1967 to only 15 instruments of ratification of the Moon Agreement of 1979. After 1979, there was no more binding international agreement. Rather, in a second phase of the space lawmaking between 1979 and 1995, we had non-binding resolutions of the United Nations General Assembly. Such resolutions included a Resolution on Direct Broadcasting by Satellites of 1982 (UNGA Res. 37/92 of 10 December 1982), the only resolution which, due to its contested character, was not adopted by unanimity but by majority; in 1986, the United Nations General Assembly Resolution on Remote Sensing by Satellite (UNGA Res. 41/65 of 3 December 1986) and in 1992, a Resolution on the use of Solar Power Sources by Satellite (UNGA Res. 47/68 of 14 December 1992). In all these cases, the members of the United Nations Committee on the Peaceful Uses of Outer Space, which is the main body preparing international space legislation, were of the opinion that a legally binding instrument should not be drafted and that non-binding resolutions would be sufficient.

In 1996, with the adoption of the famous Space Benefits Declaration (UNGA Res. 51/122 of 13 December 1996), which mainly is an interpretation of Article I, para 1 of the Outer Space Treaty, a new, third, phase of international space lawmaking started. This phase basically deals with the reinterpretation of some important notions of international space law. This was the case in 1996 with the interpretation of "space benefits" and the wording of Article I, para 1, of the Outer Space Treaty as well as was the case in 2004 with regard to the notion of "Launching State" in a new United Nations General Assembly Resolution (UNGA Res. 59/115 of 10 December 2004) and finally in 2007 with the United Nations General Assembly Resolution on "registration practice" which was an interpretation of the registration principles as contained in the Outer Space Treaty and in the Registration Convention (UNGA Res. 62/101 of 17 December 2007). Finally, in 2013, the United Nations General Assembly adopted a resolution on National Space Legislation (UNGA Res. 68/74 of 11 December 2013).

One could even go one step further and say that the current Space Debris Mitigation Guidelines as being created by the international space agencies and later supported by the United Nations General Assembly (UNGA Res. 62/217 of 22 December 2007) is yet another phase of space lawmaking. Here, the core of the normative circumscription of these principles is not even done by a United Nations body but by the national and international space agencies. At the same level is the Space Protocol to the Unidroit Convention on Asset-Based Financing, the so called Cape Town Convention, to which in 2011 a Space Protocol was added.

What does this mean? We can clearly observe a trend towards less-binding "commitments". And it is clear that these less-binding commitments are particularly for the main and major space powers. So, we are currently being on the road towards increasingly less-binding international agreements and normative solutions.

What does the International Law Require?

This does not, however, say anything yet about the existing requirements of international law concerning the national space legislation. Hence, we find a normative hook for those requirements in Article VI, sentance 2, of the Outer Space Treaty of 1967. This provision asks for authorisation and continuous supervision of national space activities by private actors. The actions of such private entities have been called permissible before in Article VI, sentence 1, of the Outer Space Treaty. So, the Outer Space Treaty demands a national authorisation and continuous supervision.

What does this mean? It means that any country from whose territory or facilities a launch is pursued or which itself or through another entity pursues an international launch needs to have a national space legislation if such a launch is to be undertaken by a private firm. Why so? The answer is relatively easy. If it would be permissible for private entities to undertake launches without any governmental authorisation and supervision, the danger would be exponentially higher in these undertakings; let's say, commercial reasons could provoke major accidents, be it in outer space, be it in the air space or be it on Earth. One would try to prevent that. And in order to also prevent states from being the only bearer of the risks of such national space activities or private space activities, it is indispensable for the internationally involved countries to implement a national space legislation. But, are countries required to adopt such national space legislation? Even if one agrees, as the present author does, on a binding force of international legal commitments, the provision of Article VI of the Outer Space Treaty does not in itself demand a national space legislation in any case. Rather, only in cases that *in concreto* a launch of a private entity is pursued from a territory, such national legislation asking for a concrete licensing of such activities is required.

What Requires International Law?

Until today, there are only a number of countries that have national space laws. Such are inter alia the United States of America, Russia, Kazakhstan, the Netherlands, the People's Republic of China, South Korea, Japan, the United Kingdom, Indonesia, South Africa, France, Ukraine, Belgium and Austria. Other important countries are missing so far—India, Germany, Spain, Brazil, Canada, etc. One should, however, clarify that any national space law must address important legal questions. These do not all follow directly from Article VI, sentance 2, of the Outer Space Treaty but go beyond that. Because, if you would take literally the Article VI of the Outer Space Treaty, you would need to implement a licensing system and the possibility and necessity of supervision.

But, taken the space codes of the various countries, one can well accept the following main points:

- authorisation (procedures and criteria)
- supervision
- liability
- insurance
- registration
- indemnification regulation

To be a bit more precise, any regime of authorisation and licensing needs to cover all activities undertaken by the natural or legal persons. In this perspective, it can be problematic what a space activity is called. Is for example the fabrication of a satellite on Earth already a space activity? There seems to be rather a kind of inclination that all activities which actualise the typical dangers of outer space (e.g. acceleration and extremely high speed) for other actors maybe called as space activities. Then of course, there is also the necessity to apply for a license that needs to be incorporated. This necessity is the fundamental point because it allows the governments to check up on personal as well as financial reliability as well as the space worthiness of the people undertaking the activities as well as the material that is being used.

Moreover, a provision should be included that answers the question of what happens in case of a transfer of the license. It would be the legal consequences of a transfer of an object in outer space.

As a next major point, the question of insurance must be regulated. Any launch by a private actor into outer space necessarily needs to be insured. This can be the showstopper for any private space activity because if there is no insurance market, the possibility of insuring against the dangers by any private activity will be reduced to almost zero. A working and well-functioning private space law should include a mandatory insurance policy. Here, the amount of the coverage is crucial. It could be for the countries an interesting point to put incentives for private actors in that only a certain amount of the damage needs to be covered by insurance and the rest would be covered by the government.

Moreover, the legislation should cover the difficult point of registration of the space object. There must be an establishment of a national registry and a provision for furnishing the information to the Secretary-General of the United Nations. What, for e.g., is the consequence of a possible double registration? The international law in the Registration Convention asks for the countries to come up with solutions in cases of double registration.

Moreover, of course, the question of supervision must be solved. Does one need a specific national law and does one need the establishment of a new supervisory authority? Can the supervisory authority be the same as the licensing authority?

In our times, it may then of course be an important point to ask for an environmental-impact assessment for any space activity of a private actor (as well as for any public actor). Moreover, there should be a clear commitment and proof that the launching entity has done everything to avoid the creation of space debris in the course of the building of a space object.

Then a provision should ask for the possibility that in case the state is being held liable according to Article VII of the Outer Space Treaty, or, respectively Articles II and III of the Liability Convention, this liable state may have recourse against the private entrepreneur.

And then, it is important to have clauses on the settlement of disputes; for example, a respective tribunal is established with its decisions being final and binding.

The International Law Association (ILA), an association of private nature that assembles approximately 4,000 lawyers around the world, has a specific Space Law Committee for which the present author has acted for more than ten years as the rapporteur. The International Law Association's Space Law Committee has worked and adopted a model law for national space legislation. It has been adopted at the biannual conference of the International Law Association in Sofia, Bulgaria, in 2012.[1] I have annexed this Model Law to my paper. This model law on national space legislation which has been adopted by the International Law Association in 2012 has a great advantage of making commentaries on the 14 articles.

---

1. ILA Res. 6/2012 on "National Space Legislation", see www.ILA/Sofia2012/Space Law Committee/Resolution. (Last Visited on 13 July 2015).

And it is not without pride, that the present author may also recall the year of 2004 when a workshop on national space legislation in the realm of a project undertaken between the Cologne Institute of Air and Space Law and the German Aerospace Center had already started to establish the so-called building blocks for national space legislation.[2]

Finally, I will mention briefly that a code was worked out at the United Nations Committee on the Peaceful Uses of Outer Space Legal Subcommittee between 2012 and 2014. It lists a number of recommendations that the launching states should take into consideration. These recommendations include the design and manufacture of spacecraft (para.1); the relevant national jurisdiction (para. 2); the requirements for authorisation and the competent national authority (para. 3); the conditions for authorisation (para. 4); the continuing supervision and enforcement (para. 5); the national registry and information by operators (para. 6); the recourse against operators and the necessary insurance (para. 7) and the continuing supervision after transfer of ownership and control in orbit (para. 8). It is an important piece of opinio juris that is likely to be supported by state practice.

Perspectives

Any modern space power that considers the necessity for more private space activities is in need of a national space law. This national space law should contain the outlined requirements; not only the 2014 UNGA Resolution but also the ILA Model Law of 2012 outline these requirements pretty well. A country like India that has already entered the arena of important space powers should therefore seriously consider having its own national space legislation. Otherwise, it risks being held liable for the activities of private entities whenever a link to India (territory, launching facility or the carrying out of a launch) can be established.

Good advice has been given in the Cologne Commentary on Space Law[3] which contains within its three volumes a commentary to almost all the questions of international space law. Moreover, advice from the Cologne Institute of Air and Space Law can at all times be reached. Annex: ILA Model Law.

---

2. Stephan Hobe, Bernhard Schmidt Tedd and Kai-Uwe Schrogl, "National Space Legislation" in *Project 2001 Plus, Towards a Harmonized Approach for National Space Legislation in Europe*, Cologne 2004.

3. Stephan Hobe, Bernhard Schmidt Tedd and Kai-Uwe Schrogl (eds.), *Cologne Commentary on Space Law*, 3 vols., Cologne 2009, 2013 and 2015. The third volume of 2015 contains all the important UNGA resolutions with a relevant commentary.

4.   Commercialisation of Remote Sensing and Geo-Spatial Data: The Emerging Legal Jargons

V. BALAKISTA REDDY

Introduction

Remote Sensing (RS) is the science of identification of the earth's surface characteristics and provides an approximate idea of their geo-biophysical properties using electromagnetic radiation which is nothing but a medium of interaction. In simple terms, remote sensing essentially deals with the obtaining of information regarding an area or object existing on the earth's surface by observing it from outer space using satellites. This activity works basically in two ways. Firstly, this device senses all the energy-packed areas of a particular territory, thus revealing different shapes and various other data which cannot be accumulated due to an impossibility of the physical presence of a person. Secondly, it works by sending the energy beams to a particular target territory and when those beams revert back, the remote sensing device records the data and accordingly produces the result giving the full information for that inaccessible place. Thus, by remote sensing, humankind can get the full, but not the entirely accurate information, without initiating physical contact with the geographical area under scrutiny.

Various satellites are launched for acquiring the remotely sensed data and to link up the communication networks. The data so acquired is usually in digital form which thereafter is processed to the required data format and subsequently is interpreted by the analysts. The interpreted satellite data may be used for identification, estimation and monitoring of various natural resources and climate forecasting, etc. by both the governmental and private entities and individuals. With the advancement in science and technology in the field of remote sensing applications, a sovereign state's territory can be sensed without the state's prior knowledge or consent which may be sometimes against the sovereignty of a state often, causing threats to national security and privacy.

A geographic information system (GIS) on the other hand is a computer-generated software which can be used for mapping and analysing the information collected through the remote sensing applications. The

GIS technology integrates common database operations, such as query and statistical analysis, with maps. It also manages location-based information and provides tools for display and analysis of various statistics, including population characteristics, economic development opportunities and vegetation types. GIS allows you to link databases and maps to create dynamic displays. Additionally, it provides tools to visualise, query, and overlay those databases in ways not possible with traditional spreadsheets. These abilities distinguish GIS from other information systems, and make it valuable to a wide range of public and private enterprises for explaining events, predicting outcomes and planning strategies.

Remote sensing data applications and geographic information systems (GIS) have an established history of interdependency. GIS provides a format to distribute the remote sensing data and to create a valuable information from the data. Remotely sensed data is also a critical means to create base GIS maps and for updating many data layers in a GIS. The integration of remotely sensed data and GIS is particularly attractive because conversion of remotely sensed raster-format data to GIS vector-format data is inexpensive and the remote sensing data offers a cost-effective way to visualise the large geographic areas in a digital format.

With the proliferation of the geographic information systems in both industry and government for numerous applications, there has been a tremendous increase in demand for remote sensing as a data input source for spatial database development. Information derived from remote sensing is particularly attractive for the GIS database development because it can provide a cost-effective and large area coverage in digital format that can be input directly into a GIS.

The remote sensing technology and GIS has been increasingly used for military reconnaissance systems and gradually for exploiting the space for scientific purposes. Their crucial role in meteorology, disaster warning and natural resource survey and management activities, etc. is well known. At present, there is an active involvement of the private sector leading to a rapid commercialisation of the information obtained through remote sensing.

Remote sensing was a revolutionary discovery which led humankind to gather information and knowledge about the different geographical units which were inaccessible and unknown to them.

The international legal framework for international space law which was also applicable to remote sensing developed way back in 1967 with the conclusion of the Outer Space Treaty 1967 followed by the

Registration Convention 1968 and the Liability Convention in 1972 and the subsequent international space legislations. These conventions operate as a general body of the international space laws applying to remote sensing with an emphasis on the major international space law principles i.e.

- Outer space activities must abide by the principles of international law
- Sovereignty cannot be evoked in relation to outer space
- Exploration and use of outer space must target the welfare and interests of all countries in whatever stage of development
- All States must be allowed an unrestricted access to outer space on equitable and non-discriminatory conditions
- Principle of Protection and Preservation of International Peace and Security and International Cooperation
- Principle of Transparency and Necessary Disclosures by way of informing the UN Secretary-General of the nature of outer space activities as well as the place where they will be performed and the ensuing effects.

However, this was a general framework for every outer space activity including remote sensing. In the favourite subject and agenda for the COPUOS discussions, after 1968, a turn can be seen in the usage of remote sensing activity from spy satellites to civilian use, and consequently the Principles relating to remote sensing of the Earth from space were developed. The most important landmark in this decade was the adoption in 1986 of the UN Principles on the Observation of Earth from Space following fifteen years of patient work by the Legal Subcommittee of COPUOS.[1]

These Principles resulted from a compromise between the actors involved, given the impossibility of reaching the agreement on an international binding instrument on the subject. In adopting these Principles, the UN returned to the method of consensus which—after a long-standing tradition within COPUOS—had been abandoned in 1982 on the occasion of the adoption of the Principles governing the Use by States of Artificial Earth Satellites for International Direct Television Broadcasting, which was decided by a majority vote.[2]

---

1.   The UN Principles Relating to Remote Sensing of the Earth from Outer Space, G.A. Res. 41/65, U.N. GAOR, 41't Sess. 95' plen. mtg., princ. I. (a), U.N. Doc.A/RES/41/65 (adopted without vote on 3 December 1986).
2.   UNGA Resolution 37/92.

The paper is divided into five subchapters covering various legal aspects of the international legal regime governing Remote Sensing and Geospatial Information Systems. It is pertinent to note at this juncture that at present there is no specific legal regime dedicated towards the Geospatial Information Systems and the data gathered through the said source. However, apart from the International Space Law treaties, the UN Principles of Remote Sensing is the nearest legal regime which can be made applicable to the data collected and traded through GIS.

The first subchapter provides with a brief overview of the historical background behind the development of the legal regime of remote sensing. The second subchapter provides the readers with a bird's-eye view of the UN Principles of Remote Sensing and the key features of the said principles. The third subchapter provides the critical assessment of the effectiveness of the international space law regimes in governing the remote sensing activities with a special focus on the UN Principles of Remote Sensing. The fourth subchapter deals with the grey areas that are yet to be resolved and are beyond the control and regulation of the international regime for Remote Sensing. The final subchapter of the paper deals with a conclusion of the arguments presented throughout the paper.

Historical Development
The history of remote sensing starts from the year 1959 when the US launched the Discoverer series which was followed by the SAMOS (i.e., Satellite and Missile Observation System), also known as the Area Surveillance System. The very first successful flight of SAMOS was made in 1961, which was supposed to be a spying satellite initiative. In response to this, the former Soviet Union launched a remote sensing satellite called Cosmos 4 in 1962. All the subsequent technological developments resulted in the "deployment of full-fledged operational reconnaissance systems for gathering data all over the world". Therefore, it can be said that the US and the former Soviet Union started to develop and deploy satellite-based reconnaissance systems to observe each other's military installations and missile deployments.

Thus, the intention behind the usage of remote sensing till the year 1968 can be said to have been motivated by the intentions of spying and unauthorised data gathering, primarily in the politico-military field.

After 1968, a turn can be seen in the usage of remote sensing activity from spy satellites to civilian use. The resultant debate was because of the controversial implications of this technology. Different sovereign nations seriously started talking about it in the first Conference on Space organised by the United Nations in Vienna in 1968. By the year 1969, the Committee on Peaceful Uses of Outer Space (COPUOS) initiated a study on international cooperation in remote sensing on the request of the UN General Assembly. COPUOS in 1970 referred the same matter to its scientific and technical subcommittee by the approval of the UN General Assembly. The General Assembly also demanded the establishment of a subcommittee by the year 1971 in order to discuss the legal issues by the working group. This subcommittee of the working group submitted a detailed report about the capabilities of remote sensing to provide an information of value in the management of natural resources.

After a decade and a half, on the recommendation of COPUOS, the Principles of Remote Sensing of Earth by Satellites were adopted by the UN General Assembly (Resolution 41/65) in the year 1986. It has to be noted that this resolution was passed unanimously. These principles were fifteen in number, and included not only a lot of ground but also provisions to respect the rights of the sensed and the sensing State. It also included the measures to enhance cooperation between the States by giving an elaborate list of responsibilities of the sensing States. This principle had also included a dispute resolution system.

While deciding the principles, a lot of issues were discussed regarding the prior consent of the sensed country, prior consultation between the sensed and the sensing country, an equal access to the information gathered from the sensed country by third parties and the legality of information gathered by the remote sensing activities considering the national sovereignty of the sensed country.

Overview of the International Legal Framework on Remote Sensing and GIS

The Principles relating to Remote Sensing of the Earth from the Outer Space is an annex to the United Nations General Assembly Resolution 41/65 adopted unanimously on December 9, 1986. At present, this document is the only specific international reference in existence on the regulation of remote sensing. The UN Remote Sensing Principles are recommendatory in nature and are not legally binding unlike the other international agreements.

The policy and legal regimes for managing the varieties of spatial data in their usage, access to them and their commercial potential however are underdeveloped and unclear. Ownership of the digital spatial data, protection of privacy, access rights to spatial data compiled and held by governments and information liability are still developing in the context of images and GIS.

This section provides a brief overview of the key provisions of the UN Principles of Remote Sensing.

The Remote Sensing Principles "establish general regulatory norms of conduct" for those remote sensing activities that relate to natural resource management, land use and the protection of the environment. They also lay out certain duties for the States that are conducting sensing activities as well as the rights of those States that are being sensed. These include the duty to consult with the States being sensed as well as an obligation to share data with the sensed States on a non-discriminatory basis.[3]

The Remote Sensing Principles are seen as being a particularly useful as a first step in the establishment of a wider range of tools and cooperative measures. For example, the provisions in the Remote Sensing Principles on "protection of the Earth's environment" and "protection of mankind from all natural disasters" have led to the adoption of the Charter in Cooperation to Achieve the Coordinated Use of Space Facilities in the Event of Natural or Technological Disasters, an instrument aimed at providing a unified system of data acquisition and delivery to those affected by natural or manmade disasters.[4] The Remote Sensing Principles have also been incorporated into numerous national, regional, and multilateral laws and policies, including those of France, Japan, India, Thailand and the United States of America.[5] Such developments demonstrate the potential value of such norms in building the subsequent national and international frameworks and for informing the development of national space activities and their regulation.

Purpose of Remote Sensing Activities

Reiterating the customary norm of the international space law, Principle II provides for the underlying principles in the light of which the Remote Sensing activities are required to be conducted i.e. for the benefit and in the interests of all countries, irrespective of their degree of economic, social or scientific and technological development, and taking into particular

---

3. F. von der Dunk, *United Nations Principles on Remote Sensing and the User*, 2002, pp. 36-37, 39-40, and J.I. Gabrynowicz, "The UN Principles Relating to Remote Sensing of the Earth" in I. Marboe (ed.), *Soft Law in Outer Space: The Function of Non-Binding Norms in International Space Law*, 2012, p. 189.
4. Ibid., p. 191.
5. Ibid., pp.189-190.

consideration the needs of the developing countries.[6] The very general reference to the benefit and interests of all countries especially with a special focus on the developing countries is also a general treaty-making practice followed in the international legal framework. In order to clarify the extent of discretion that the nations have while determining the benefit and interest of all countries, the UN passed a resolution in 1996 to specifically deal with a further interpretation and elaboration of this concept. But, it ended up giving the states the complete freedom to "to determine all aspects" of such cooperation, further repeatedly referring to the requirement of "an equitable and mutually acceptable basis" for any activities undertaken in its implementation.[7]

Underlying Principles of Remote Sensing

Remote sensing activities shall be conducted in accordance with international law, including the Charter of the United Nations, the Treaty on Principles Governing the Activities of States in the Exploration and Use of Outer Space, including the Moon and Other Celestial Bodies, and the relevant instruments of the International Telecommunication Union.[8] This principle lays down the underlying principle and subjects the remote sensing activities to the customary norms of international law including the UN Charter, the Outer Space Treaty and the relevant legal instruments developed by the International Telecommunication Union (ITU).

This safety-net clause in practice is largely relevant for the space part of remote sensing activities. This is the consequence of the fact that international law plays its largest role in outer space where no single state can exercise comprehensive—that is territorial—jurisdiction, with the ensuing legal control over the activities undertaken there.

Respecting the Sovereignty of States

Besides repeating the aforesaid principles, the next principle further provides that these activities shall be conducted on the basis of respect for the principle of full and permanent sovereignty of all States and peoples over their own wealth and natural resources, with due regard to the rights and interests, in

---

6. *Supra* Note 1, Principle II.
7. Declaration on International Cooperation in the Exploration and Use of Outer Space for the Benefit and in the Interest of all States, Taking into Particular Account the Needs of Developing Countries, UNGA Res. 51/122, of 13 December 1996; XXII-I Annals of Air and Space Law (1997), at 556; 46 Zeitschrift fur Luft- und Weltraumrecht (1997), at 236.
8. *Supra* Note 1, Principle III.

accordance with international law, of other States and entities under their jurisdiction. Such activities shall not be conducted in a manner detrimental to the legitimate rights and interests of the sensed State.[9]

This principles strike directly at the heart of one of the core issues of remote sensing i.e. achieving a balance between the freedom of use of outer space in its particular manifestation of freedom of information and the principle of sovereignty of states over their own territory—more in particular over their own wealth and natural resources. The principle protects the sovereignty of the sensed states and secures the interests of all the countries. All this, however, does not alter the fact that the "sensed state" has no veto to prevent it from being "sensed" or even an exclusive, free, or preferential right of access to the data. This becomes especially clear when this Principle is seen in conjunction with Principles XII and XIII.

Principle of International Cooperation

A key element of the remote sensing regime is the emphasis on the cooperation to which the Principles V, VIII and XIII are devoted. They mention the obligation of the sensing States to promote international cooperation and to make available to other States opportunities for participation on equitable and mutually acceptable terms, the obligation of the UN and relevant agencies of the UN system to promote cooperation—including the technical assistance and coordination in the area of remote sensing—the promotion of international cooperation especially with regards to the needs of the developing countries by the means of consultations upon request with the sensed States.

State practice has given strong support to the cooperation principles. States and IOs have entered into agreements to jointly finance the satellite systems for monitoring the earth's environment. This kind of cooperation has become essential not only in expanding the availability of space technology and applications so that all countries may benefit from them but also mainly in promoting the international security in all its forms.

This principle has been reasserted in the Benefits Declaration which is applicable to the Outer Space Treaty as well.

Establishment of Data Collecting and Storage Stations

In order to maximise the availability of benefits from the remote sensing activities, States are encouraged, through agreements or other arrangements,

---

9. *Supra* Note 1, Principle IV.

to provide for the establishment and operation of data collecting and storage stations and processing and interpretation facilities, in particular within the framework of regional agreements or arrangements wherever feasible.[10] The principle is extremely crucial as it hints towards the development of an enforcement mechanism at the national level for the purposes of an effective implementation of the UN Principles on Remote Sensing. However, it ends up encouraging the states to establish the necessary mechanism and this in conjunction with the principled lack of binding force will not readily result in many States establishing the relevant rules on a (private) user level.

Principle of Technical Assistance on Mutually Agreed Terms

States participating in remote sensing activities shall make available technical assistance to other interested States on mutually agreed terms.[11] Being little more than an extension of or complement to Principle VI, the same reasoning applies to this Principle, urging the sharing of technical knowledge but it comes with a rider of mutually agreed terms.

UN and International Cooperation

The United Nations and the relevant agencies within the United Nations system shall promote international cooperation, including technical assistance and coordination in the area of remote sensing.[12] It sketches the desired measure of involvement of the United Nations system in promoting the aims of the Resolution in rather broad and vague terms thereby leaving the scope and extent of the UN involvement to the absolute discretion of the organisation.

Principle of Transparency and Necessary Disclosures and Protection of Earth's Environment

A general clause is enshrined under Principle IX setting forth the obligation of information concerning the remote sensing programme as a whole that the sensing state is carrying out. The following principles i.e. Principle X and IX deal with environmental harm.

Principle IX lays down the fundamental norm of transparency as enshrined under the International Space Law Treaties obligating the States to inform the UN Secretary-General of the nature of the outer space activities

---

10.   Ibid., Principle VI.
11.   Ibid., Principle VII.
12.   Ibid., Principle VIII.

as well as the place where they will be performed and the ensuing effects.[13] Principle X imposes upon the States participating in the remote sensing activities if having identified the information in their possession capable of averting any phenomenon harmful to the earth's natural environment, to disclose such information to the States concerned. The second provides for the duty of prompt transmission to the affected States of the collected data and of the information relating to national emergencies. Principle XI further obligates the States participating in the remote sensing activities and in pursuance of which they have identified the processed data and analysed the information regarding any impending natural disasters, to inform the potential States which may be affected by such information.

Though the language of the Principles X and XI might resemble, however it is pertinent to note that the applicability of the two is different yet interconnected. While Principle X is concerned with human-origin threats to the natural environment of the Earth, Principle XI focuses on nature's threats to humankind. Another noticeable difference is that Principle XI is more detailed in explicitly applying the "processed data" in addition to "analysed information", as opposed to mere "information."

Information promoting environmental protection is therefore given a different status vis-à-vis the access to data regime as set forth in Principle XII.

Right of Access to Data by the Sensed State

As soon as the primary data and the processed data concerning the territory under its jurisdiction is produced, the sensed State shall have access to them on a non-discriminatory basis and on reasonable cost terms. The sensed State shall also have access to the available analysed information concerning the territory under its jurisdiction in the possession of any State participating in remote sensing activities on the same basis and terms, with a particular regard being given to the needs and interests of the developing countries.[14]

The sensed State has no right to prevent itself from being sensed, however, it certainly has a right, at least in principle, to gain access to such data "on a non-discriminatory basis and on reasonable cost terms." The nature and location of the data does not affect the legality of such gathered information, rather it solely depends on the place from which the data is gathered since it might amount to interference in the internal affairs of the sensed country.

---

13. Ibid., Principle IX.
14. Ibid., Principle XII

In furtherance of this principle, the next principle encourages the States to promote and intensify international cooperation, especially with regard to the needs of the developing countries; a State carrying out a remote sensing of the Earth from space shall, upon request, enter into consultations with a State whose territory is sensed in order to make available opportunities for participation and for enhancing the mutual benefits to be derived therefrom.[15] However, if consultations do not lead to a negotiated outcome acceptable to both parties, there would be no "obligation for the "sensing State" to treat the "sensed State" any better than it does the other States interested in these data.

International Responsibility for Remote Sensing Activities

In compliance with Article VI of the Outer Space Treaty, the States operating the remote sensing satellites shall bear international responsibility for their activities and assure that such activities are conducted in accordance with the provisions of the Treaty and the norms of international law, irrespective of whether such activities are carried out by governmental or non-governmental entities or through international organisations to which such States are parties. This principle is without prejudice to the applicability of the norms of international law on State responsibility for remote sensing activities.[16]

The principle as mentioned above includes both governmental and nongovernmental entities including private entities within its ambit and makes them internationally responsible for their indulgence in remote sensing activities. Under this Principle, a State should be held responsible on the international level for those private entities undertaking remote sensing activities which either operate from its territory or have its nationality.

Peaceful Settlement of Disputes

Any dispute resulting from the application of these principles shall be resolved through the established procedures for the peaceful settlement of disputes.[17] The whole Resolution being State-oriented, the "established procedures" referred to are State-to-State procedures such as diplomatic negotiation, mediation, conciliation, arbitration and recourse to an international tribunal or court having jurisdiction. For the private entities involved in the space part

---

15. Ibid., Principle XIII
16. Ibid., Principle XIV.
17. Ibid., Principle XV.

of the remote sensing operations, the consequences of this State-oriented dispute settlement mechanism might be quite severe, since it might preclude in many ways solutions to the conflicts that are fair to the private parties.

Critical Assessment of the International Legal Framework

Definitions of Remote Sensing and Remote Sensing Activities
The 1986 Principles distinguish three types of information:
- Primary data: this is acquired by remote sensors borne by a space object and transmitted or delivered to the ground by telemetry in the form of electromagnetic signals, photographic films or magnetic tapes or any other means.
- Processed data: it means the products resulting from the processing of primary data, needed to make these data usable.
- Analysed Information: This results from an interpretation of the processed data, inputs of data and knowledge from other sources.[18]

According to the UN RS Principles, RS does not embrace all forms of Earth's observation. Rather, it embraces all those activities which are conducted in order to improve the management of natural resources, the use of land and the protection and preservation of the environment thereby ultimately aiming towards the realisation of the prime object of sustainable development and not profitable or political motives. Therefore, the military or commercial activities regarding the information obtained through Remote Sensing and GIS would be beyond the scope of this Principle.

Nevertheless, the five major outer space treaties and their respective relevant customary norms are applicable to all the State's activities carried out in outer space, including other remote sensing activities. If we analyse closely the UN Remote Sensing Principles, it can be noticed that these principles are nothing but a reiteration of the general rules of international space law.

Responsibility for Remote Sensing Activities
Principle XIV deals with one of the most controversial provision of the document and provides for a dual system of responsibility in order to cover both types of remote sensing. According to the first part of Principle XIV, States operating the remote sensing satellites shall bear international responsibility for their activities and assure that such activities are conducted

18. Ibid., Principle I.

in accordance with the principles and norms of international law, irrespective of whether such activities are being carried out by governmental or private entities. This reiterates Article VI of the OST and Article VII of the LC and as a result provides for a victim-oriented discipline of absolute responsibility or strict liability for the damages caused by space objects on the surface of the earth or to aircraft flight.

Most of the spacefaring nations have developed domestic legislations in conformity with Article VI of the OST which explicitly obligate the member states to control and supervise activities carried out on earth and in outer space. The latter segment of the principle contains a very controversial aspect of the provisions following which the forgoing principles are without prejudice to the applicability of the norms of international law on State Responsibility for remote sensing activities, that is to say, the activities carried out also on earth. This proviso enumerates the rules of customary international law for private conduct and the State by virtue of its very nature is responsible for having neglected to take all the reasonable measures to prevent the offensive acts from being committed. It can be thus argued that the remote sensing activities carried out by the private entities on earth are to be considered as a form of conduct directed or controlled by the State under Article 8 of the ILC Draft Articles and as such, attributable to the State concerned.

Thus, while remote sensing, the State's absolute responsibility for private national activities in outer space is subjected to the special regime set forth in Article VI of the 1967 OST and the 1972 LC; the State's responsibility for any wrongful act as foreseen by the general international law can originate from the remote sensing national private activities carried out on earth.

Principles reiterating the Treaty or Customary International Rules

Principle III contains a very general rule according to which the Remote Sensing Activities shall be conducted in accordance with the international law including the Charter of the United Nations, the OST and the relevant instruments of the ITU. Principle IX recalls the duties of the State under Article IV of the Registration Convention and Article IX of the OST to inform the UNSG.

The principle springs from the fundamental principle of common benefit of humankind in the freedom of exploration and the use of outer space on the basis of equality.

At this juncture, it is pertinent to note that the right of the States, IO and nongovernmental entities to engage in remote sensing activities is not explicitly stated in the GA Resolution or Principles but, nevertheless, the said right is considered to be the cornerstone of the remote sensing international legal regime. At the time of the adoption of the principles, the Principles did not object or prohibit any sensing activity which had been going on for a substantial period of time. On the contrary, they accepted the fact that the sensing activities required no consent, not even from the sensed states. Therefore, the Principles merely codify a well-established conduct of the States.

Right to Disseminate Remote Sensing Information:

The legality of dissemination of the satellite imagery has been the subject of controversy in the COPUOS for over two decades. There essentially were two opposing views: one stressed sovereignty in the form of the freedom of action of the sensing State and the other pleaded sovereignty over the natural resources of the sensed State. The first view was presented by the States (i.e. the US and some of the Western countries) that advocated the unrestricted use of satellites for remote sensing and the freedom of distribution of satellite imagery. The second view, advanced mainly by the Socialist and developing countries, stressed that the reception, processing and distribution of the imagery acquired with the satellites are essentially earth-based activities and thus must be governed by State sovereignty, especially the universally recognised principle[19] of permanent sovereignty over the natural resources within a State's territorial jurisdiction.[20] They advocated the need of a prior consent of the sensed State for distribution of the satellite imagery to third State(s). This view was well expressed by the then Soviet Union and was strongly supported by the developing countries.[21]

This view was not shared by other delegations to the COPUOS. However, after lengthy discussions there, the UN General Assembly, on the recommendation of the COPUOS in 1986, finally adopted unanimously a Resolution containing the Principles Relating to Remote Sensing of the Earth from Outer Space.[22]

---

19. Declaration on Permanent Sovereignty over Natural Resources, G.A. Res. 1803 (XVII), U.N. GAOR (1962).

20. This principle is considered to have become a part of the jus cogens applicable to all States. See Brownlie, supra note 30, at 515; Brownlie, Ian, *Principles of Public International Law*, pp. 446-447 (1998).

21. UN Doc. A/AC.105/C.2/L.99 (1974).

22. The UN Principles Relating to Remote Sensing of the Earth from Outer Space, G.A. Res. 41/65, U.N. GAOR, 41't Sess. 95' plen. mtg., princ. I. (a), U.N. Doc.A/RES/41/65 (adopted without vote on 3 December 1986).

The Resolution recognises the interests of the sensed State(s) as it provides that remote sensing activities,[23]

"..shall be conducted on the basis of respect for the principle of full and permanent sovereignty of all States and peoples over their own wealth and natural resources, with due regard to the rights and interests, in accordance with international law, of other States and entities under their jurisdiction. Such activities shall not be conducted in a manner detrimental to the legitimate rights and interests of the sensed State."

However, it is nowhere mentioned in the Resolution that the sensing State should seek the consent or authorisation of the sensed State prior to the distribution of the imagery acquired with the use of a satellite. As noted earlier, the principle of full and permanent sovereignty of all States over their natural resources is a principle of customary international law. However, the information about these resources acquired by remote sensing satellites becomes the property of the sensing State, which remains free to use or disseminate this information. Moreover, it should be kept in mind that the State of Registry retains the jurisdiction, control and ownership over its satellites launched into outer space[24] and consequently over the benefits accrued, including the imagery acquired with the use of satellite(s). In other words, the right of control over and the ownership of the satellite imagery are based on the principle of State sovereignty[25], though within the parameters of international law. Thus, a State, in its relations with others, is authorised to both positive and negative rights over its property (including the property belonging to its nationals); i.e. a State can use or dispose of its property as well as not to use or not to distribute it to others.

India is trying to control the distribution of satellite imagery but to its own nationals. Under a July 2000 agreement between the Government of India and the Space Imaging Company of the US, "sensitive Indian installations

---

23. The term "remote sensing activities" as defined by Principle I (para f) of the UN Resolution on Remote Sensing means "the operation of remote sensing space systems, primary data collection and storage stations, and activities in processing, interpreting and disseminating the processed data". Ibid.
24. Article VIII, Outer Space Treaty.
25. State sovereignty implies the existence and the freedom of action of the States, as limited by international law, in their international relations as well as with respect to their internal affairs; especially, the freedom of an exclusive jurisdiction over their territory, their personal jurisdiction over their citizens and the legal persons established under their jurisdiction, things present and matters happening in their jurisdiction.

such as military bases and airfields will be blotted out of Ikonos images before they are distributed" in India. The usefulness and effectiveness of this approach are questionable.[26] However, this example provides a further evidence of the State practice to control the distribution of satellite imagery at least about its own territory and to its own nation.

Right to seek Information from the Sensing State:

Does the sensed State have a right under international law to seek or demand from the sensing State the satellite imagery or other relevant information of its own territory which has been obtained by the sensing State with the help of the remote sensing and GIS applications? In this regard, Principle XII provides us with some answers. However, the general language and loose terms of the provisions has left open many ambiguities which are subjected to contradictory interpretations. Although as per the principles, the sensed state has a right to demand the satellite imagery about its territory, nevertheless this right is merely in the nature of a moral right given the guiding nature of the principles. Nevertheless, the principle of non-discriminatory access has been cited by various nations and their entities as an authoritative principle applicable to their satellite imagery distribution policies.[27]

The aforesaid principle of the UN Principles of Remote Sensing 1982 explicitly recognises the legal right of the sensed State to seek from the sensing State the satellite imagery of its own territory. While the Resolution has accepted the position of the Western States by recognising the right of the sensing State to acquire the satellite imagery without the consent of the sensed State, it has also incorporated the position taken by the Socialist and developing countries as it recognises their interests in having a non-discriminatory access to the satellite imagery of their respective territories.[28] It is therefore expected of the sensing State(s) to positively respond to the requests by the sensed States for a satellite imagery of their respective territories.

---

26. "India's Futile Imagery Policy", *Space News*, July 24, 2000, at 22.
27. US Land Remote Sensing Policy Act of 1992 (5601-5642; Canadian RADARSAT Data Policy, Document no. RSCA-PROO04, Sec. 10.1 b., (Canadian Space Agency), July 13, 1994, at 11; ESA Envisat Data Policy, ESA/PB-EO (97) rev. 3, Paris, (European Space Agency), 19 Feb. 98; Principles of the Provision of ERS Data to Users, ESA/PB-EO (90) 57, rev. 6 Paris, 9 May 1994, (European Space Agency, Earth Observation Programme Board), Sec. 2 General Principles, 2.1 Legal Principles, para. 2, at 2).
28. Stephan Gorove, "Developments in Space Law: Issues and Policies", 10 Utrecht Studies in Air and Space Law, LAW 300 (1991).

However, this right has a very restricted scope because of many reasons. Firstly, the right belongs to only accessing of the satellite imagery acquired for "the purpose of improving natural resources management, land use and the protection of the environment'. This does not include the imagery for meteorological and military purposes. Moreover, the phrase 'Non-discriminatory access on reasonable cost terms' has not been defined, thereby leaving the meaning and their extent very ambiguous leading to inconsistent interpretations. To begin with, the phrase 'reasonable costs' has not been defined anywhere. Going by the standard definitions of the term, it can either indicate marginal costs or market price in so far as it is reasonable for the particular data in question.

At this juncture, one may revert to the disclosure obligation under Principle X and XI of the UN Principles. However, these principles also fail to state the on what terms the data should be supplied in such cases. Therefore, they do not serve as a legal basis to allow the data use and sharing for public benefit purposes at favourable conditions.

Emerging Legal Concerns in the International Legal Framework for Remote Sensing and GIS

The principles have been surpassed by the skyrocketing technological advances in the sector that have occurred in the last few decades. In the light of these technological advances, the existing legal regime has fallen short of addressing the many grey issues that have emerged in the contemporary times with the growing usage of multiple satellite remote sensing programmes, especially when a large part of them is being operated with strictly commercial and profit-making motives. The high-resolution images that were until recently being exclusively used by the armed forced for the purposes of national security are being presently sold worldwide.

Due to political complexities, the Remote Sensing Principles refrain from addressing certain legal questions, such as whether a state has a proprietary right to the images of its own natural resources.[29] The restricted language also means that the provisions of the principles will need to be amended in order to take into account the emergence of new technological capabilities, such as long-term earth monitoring.[30]

---

29. H. Desaussure, "Remote Sensing Satellite Regulation by National and International Law", 15 *Rutgers Computer and Tech Law Journal*, vol. 15, no. 1, 1989, pp. 357, 374.

30. J.I. Gabrynowicz, "The UN Principles relating to Remote Sensing of the Earth" in I. Marboe (ed.), *Soft Law in Outer Space: The Function of Non-Binding Norms in International Space Law*, 2012, p. 190.

The first and foremost flaw in this regime is that it is in the nature of guiding principles and not that of a binding international agreement. This reduces the enumerated obligation to only a merely morally binding one on the member nations.

Combining the Civil and Military Remote Sensing Programmes

Lately, many states have tried to merge the civil and military remote sensing programmes. The Presidential Directive of United States of 1994 has been once of the glaring instances of the said ambiguity. This directive, in essence, has enforced a combination of the military and civilian programmes of the meteorological satellites in the Polar orbit including the noble objective of environmental monitoring. Here, the convergence was based on the principles of the recognised significance of the operational environmental data and an assured data access, which would further give the possible power to selectively deny the critical environmental data during a political crisis or conflicts for security reasons. Since the launch of the first remote sensing satellite in 1960, significant technological advances have been made as active satellites are now being routinely launched and used; imagery of one metre resolution is readily available and a highly accurate information is being derived by using the sophisticated data interpretation techniques and expertise. A large number of remote sensing satellites are currently in orbit and more are expected to be launched in the near future. They currently provide and will continue providing imagery at various details for numerous civil and military applications.[31] Since the end of the Cold War, military remote sensing technology and techniques are being increasingly applied for civilian applications. Consequently, the capabilities of the civil remote sensing satellites are increasing to such an extent that they can now be applied to military tasks to a large extent. Besides the better resolution of the modern systems on board the satellites, another significant improvement has been the ability to point the camera sideways.

There are numerous applications of satellite imagery both for civilian and military purposes. The civilian uses could include: meteorology and weather forecasting, crop monitoring, pollution monitoring and environmental protection, cartography and land use, marine and earth resources discovery and management, natural disaster assistance, news gathering, etc. Military applications of the satellite imagery include: reconnaissance, missile launch

---

31. For a detailed information on the numerous remote sensing satellite systems belonging to various countries, visit: http://www.fas.org/spp/uide/index.html (date accessed: 6/11/00).

detection, arms control treaty verification, strategic and tactical planning, etc. Increased capabilities of the civilian remote sensing satellites and the ready availability of the commercial sources of satellite imagery are fast developing both newer applications and a huge worldwide market. However, these developments have started giving rise to security concerns as well.

In spite of all the interpretations and efforts to demilitarise outer space, the military use and exploration of space has been occurring since the beginning even before the Outer Space Treaty took effect in 1967—and it does not seem to be heading towards an end. Since the remote sensing data became commercially available, individuals have been able to acquire any sort of images and data obtained from the remote sensing systems.

Commercialisation of remote sensing poses more of a threat to the countries than the militarisation of space. States are in a constant fight to provide their citizens with the tranquility that their rights will not be violated. However, individuals might not be able to assimilate the responsibility that comes with the access to an endless amount of information. The use of remotely sensed data by the wrong people can become a problem of national security. Do the countries have a higher duty to protect their citizens' rights or their well-being?

Commercialisation of the Remote Sensing Activities
The decade of the nineties was identified with a sharp move towards the commercial space activities. The participation of the private companies in the use of outer space was now giving way to a more complex but clearer scenario, both from the legal and political standpoints.

Currently, the potential commercialisation of remote sensing is limitless. Today, almost all advances in the remote sensing technology have civil and military applications since at its beginning, remote sensing was primarily used in the reconnaissance satellites for the military.[32] The remote sensing technology is still generally being used for agricultural and environmental studies, terrain mapping and a new market for remote sensed imagery is being developed in the real estate market where companies are offering photographs of homes, neighbourhoods and traffic patterns taken from space.[33] Currently, individuals can even use their home computers to view a high resolution imagery of certain places. In addition, it can be argued that

---

32. Captain Michael R. Hoversten, "US National Security and Government Regulation of Commercial Remote Sensing from Outer Space", 50 A.F. L. REv. 253, 260 (2001) at p. 253.
33. Susan M. Jackson, "Cultural Lag and the International Law of Remote Sensing", 23 *Brook J. INT'L L*, 853, 858 (1998) at pp. 856-57.

any photograph of the earth taken from space can be used for both civilian and military purposes. Further, communication satellites used to transport communication for civilian purposes can also be used to transport military communications in times of war.[34] And since it has been established that States cannot prohibit the placement of remote sensing satellites in space that will take the images of their territory, all remotely sensed images are up for grabs—whether it is by the military, an individual, or a private corporation.[35]

The commercialisation of remote sensing imagery has created a great division of views. Some think that dissemination of the remotely sensed data will benefit everyone by reducing the tension caused by the search for information; others disagree and affirm that the distribution of that data can not be obtained asymmetrically by the less developed, developing and developed countries.

The first view sustains the idea that commercial dissemination will hinder the States' capabilities to keep secret their military potential and any nuclear, biological, or chemical production factories that they might have, therefore, it will discourage such countries from having these facilities. In contrast, the supporters of the second theory fear that the advances in technology plus the commercial distribution of the remotely sensed high resolution images will nourish international competition and cause the nations to attempt to destroy each other's military defences. Further, a commercial dissemination of the remote sensing imagery can increase the opportunities available for the terrorist groups to come across valuable information that could be used against a country.

The less-developed countries and the developing countries to a very large extent have constantly found themselves at a disadvantage when it comes to Remote Sensing Commercialisation. LDCs also face a great disparity in accessing the information. Even though most of the data is commercially available, there is some data that cannot be accessed in the market and these countries do not have the necessary resources to implement a remote sensing system of their own.[36] The nations do not have the right to prohibit the remote sensing systems from taking images of their territory.[37] Even

---

34. Major Douglas S. Anderson, Judge Advocate, United States Air Force, "A Military Look into Space: The Ultimate High Ground", 1995, *Army Law*, 19, 24 (Nov. 1995) at p. 27.
35. *Supra* Note 17 at p. 876.
36. T. A. Heppenheimer, "Operational Remote Sensing Satellites", http://www.centennialofflight.gov/essay/SPACEFLIGHT/remote-sensing/SP36.htm (last visited Aug. 1, 2007).
37. Outer Space Treaty, supra note 4, Article 2.

though this seems to even out the playing field, it is a disadvantage to the LDCs because their natural resources, military bases and defences are out in the open for everyone to see. Conversely, the LDCs do not have access to the most precious secrets of other nations; neither do they have the resources to buy the data for their own territories to prevent it from being disseminated.

Infringement of Privacy Rights

The Right to Privacy is one of the basic tenets of the fundamental right of Right to Life and Personnel Liberty as enshrined under the Indian Constitution.[38] The Right to Privacy as a basic fundamental right of every individual is not only in India but in almost every constitution of the world. However, the various applications of remote sensing and GIS like 'Google Earth' carry the potential to infringe the right to privacy of the individuals. Though there have not been any cases in India, but abroad this right has been constantly challenged. For example, in the Dow Chemical Co. v. U.S., decided in 1986, Dow claimed that the Environmental Protection Agency (EPA) violated Dow's Fourth Amendment rights when it hired a commercial aerial photographer to photograph one of Dow's facilities without first obtaining a warrant. The photographer used a standard mapping camera and flew within lawful airspace. The Supreme Court held that even though Dow had security walls around its complex, it did not have a reasonable expectation of privacy with respect to what was not covered behind the walls because it was "open to the view and observation of persons in aircraft lawfully in the public airspace immediately above. . ." It is worth noting however, that the Court left open the question as to whether the "surveillance of private property by using highly sophisticated surveillance equipment not generally available to the public, such as satellite technology, might be constitutionally proscribed absent a warrant."

Similarly, in California v. Ciraolo, also decided in 1986, two police officers had hired a plane to fly over a private house to see if they could see signs of marijuana being grown. The house was otherwise surrounded by a fence. Based upon a visual observation of the marijuana plants, the police obtained a warrant to search the house and subsequently seized the plants. Ciraolo's attorney argued that the flyover was an unreasonable search and seizure, because it violated its reasonable expectation of privacy with respect to his backyard. However, a majority of the Supreme Court jury disagreed, finding in part that "...in an age where private and commercial

38. The Constitution of India 1950, Article 21.

flight in the public airways is routine, it is unreasonable for respondent to expect that his marijuana plants were constitutionally protected from being observed with the naked eye from an altitude of 1,000 feet."

A few years later, in Florida v. Riley, the Supreme Court was faced with a similar set of facts. However, in this case, a sheriff used a helicopter instead of a plane to fly over a house and conduct a visual search. Based upon what he saw in the openings of a greenhouse roof and through its open sides, the official obtained a warrant and in the search found marijuana. Riley's attorney argued that the helicopter overflight violated Riley's constitutional rights in part because the helicopter did not fly at the required altitude for aircraft. However, the majority of the Supreme Court jury found that because the helicopter was within the FAA altitude requirements for a helicopter, Riley's expectation of privacy was unreasonable as he did not completely cover the marijuana from view.

Justice O'Connor's concurring opinion helps show how complex this analysis can be. She stated that the majority relied too heavily on whether the helicopter was flying in compliance with the FAA regulations. Instead, she argued that a reasonable expectation of privacy was "whether it was in the public airway at an altitude at which members of the public travel with sufficient regularity that respondent's expectation was not one that society would find reasonable." She added that observations from helicopters circling over a home may be so sufficiently rare that police surveillance from such an altitude would violate a reasonable expectation of privacy, despite a compliance with the FAA regulations.

The rapid improvements in spatial technology have challenged the legal system in a number of different ways. Privacy is certainly one of the most difficult issues. The legal system has and will continue to struggle to define privacy in a spatial context, particularly as commercial applications for satellite imagery, GPS, RFID, GIS and other technologies grow. In the meantime, courts will seek to protect privacy rights by analysing the laws that are not so easily applied to the current technology. Nevertheless, one can get a sense of the legal framework as well as the potential issues by examining how the privacy law has been interpreted and applied to the other technologies.

The GIS databases hold all kinds of geographic information relevant to specific individuals. They may include tax and land records, property titles, data on construction or occupancy permits, data on residency or on water use. Sometimes, that data might be incorrect and so may cause economic or social harm. How are the creators or keepers of the information to be held responsible for the accuracy of their information? At present, credit bureaus must provide reports to individuals in order to allow people the opportunity to rectify incorrect information. But other kinds of databases are not held at similar standards. This problem has not yet been resolved and it is becoming increasingly troubling as more and more data on private citizens is being collected and stored on computers. The possibility of inaccuracies has always existed with paper documentation, but as information is distributed, and redistributed, and stored in ever greater quantities, the ability of individuals to know who may be holding and distributing incorrect data on them becomes a more complex problem. The solution will probably come in some form of legal safeguards.

Intellectual Property Rights and Remote Sensing: Points of Intersection
Recently, remote sensing data and GIS have been variously applied to the fields of research and industry in the world. In most of cases, the database of geographic information is a big treasure belonging to a company or a government. However, the digital data set is expensive to generate but easy to copy and propagate. The private sector would be reluctant to invest a great amount of money unless profits can be expected to be made. Thus, proper protection is necessary to foster the development of this kind of information industry.

The full potential of remote sensing could not be reached with a governmentally-owned and operated remote sensing programme. Commercialisation was thus necessary for the further development of this technology. Now that commercialisation is in place, the marketing of such data needs to be maximised. For this purpose, intellectual property rights in enhanced data are necessary to increase the number of data enhancement firms and thereby increase the market for raw data.

An understanding of the application of intellectual property rights to remote sensing data requires an understanding of the difference between the enhanced and unenhanced data. Unenhanced data, or raw data, is obtained directly from the satellite and primarily consists of digital information or photographs. Enhanced data, in contrast, is the result of human or electronic analysis of the raw data.

International copyright protection for enhanced data is necessary for inducing the firms to enter the data enhancement industry. Even a small data enhancement firm must invest a significant capital in software, equipment and trained personnel before it can begin operation. Copyright laws will protect this investment and, by making the processed data more valuable, will provide an incentive for the firms to enter the market. Without the economic rents created by copyright, it is unlikely that enough firms will produce a sufficiently enhanced data to make commercialisation worthwhile. This is because the data enhancement industry will constitute the market for raw data which is necessary to realise a profit.

Competition from the foreign remote sensing systems provides another reason why a legal protection of the enhanced data is necessary. Many countries operate commercial remote sensing systems, and some of these, such as the French SPOT system and the European Space Agency's ERS-1 (both commercialised systems), compete with the US's Landsat for the international as well as the domestic data markets. A significant feature of the international intellectual property rights is that these rights shall protect competition among all entities producing the enhanced data worldwide. Without copyright protection, an individual or entity could pirate the enhanced data produced by someone else and legitimately pass it off as its own. There would be no mechanism to prevent such an entity from distorting the data to obtain financial or political benefits. Therefore, the nature of a commercial remote sensing programme mandates the copyright protection for enhanced data. Such a copyright protection will benefit the producers of enhanced data worldwide due to the existence of multilateral copyright agreements.

Although representatives from the developing nations have expressed concerns regarding the legal protection of processed data, it is conceivable that in the near future their views will change. This will occur upon the realisation that the benefits of copyright (widespread availability and low prices for unenhanced data) will outweigh the disadvantages (decreased availability of processed data). As the developing nations become capable of processing the data themselves, they may also accept the copyright due to the fact that it will protect their own processed data from theft and misappropriation by entities which might use the information to exploit the developing nations' resources. These considerations, combined with the protection of international space agreements, clearly demonstrate that the copyright protection of the enhanced remote sensing data will serve the divergent needs of both the industrialised and developing nations.

The UN Principles on Remote Sensing have failed to cater to the growing need of protecting the data thus received from the remote sensing and GIS Applications.

The Berne Convention is believed to provide the protection necessary to meet the needs of a commercial remote sensing industry. This agreement consists of two principal components. The first is the main body of the agreement which details and defines the functions and operation of international copyright protection for protected works. The second component of the Berne Convention is the appendix, which provides special mechanisms for the developing nations to gain access to the copyrighted material. This section is especially relevant to the remote sensing data which may significantly benefit the developing countries.[39]

The remote sensing imagery is part of the general scope of Article 2 of the Berne Convention. At a minimum, the Convention covers the first imagery product after the bits transmitted by the satellite have been converted into a readable photograph, which raises the question of the protection of the raw data. In order to help the copyright protection be effective, the Berne Convention provides that the works must be "fixed in some material form" and that the national laws may not renege on their obligation to participate in such protection. Only the news information is not covered by these provisions.[40]

The extent to which an automatic protection is afforded to the author is determined by the Convention in association with the country where

---

39. West, J. Richard, "Copyright Protection for Data Obtained by Remote Sensing: How the Data Enhancement Industry will ensure Access for Developing Countries", 11 Nw. J. Int'l L. & Bus. 403 (1990) at http//: international.westlaw.com (last visited Oct 17, 2005).

40. Excerpts from Article 5, Berne Convention: "(1) Authors shall enjoy, in respect of works for which they are protected under this Convention, in countries of the Union other than the country of origin, the rights which their respective laws do now or may hereafter grant to their nationals, as well as the rights specially granted by this Convention. (2) The enjoyment and the exercise of these rights shall not be subject to any formality ... the extent of protection, as well as the means of redress afforded to the author to protect his rights, shall be governed exclusively by the laws of the country where protection is claimed ...". Convention for the Protection of Literary and Artistic Works, 63 U.K.T.S. 29 (1990); as quoted in infra n. xxiii.

the protection is sought.[41] The amount of protection which is granted to a foreign work is based on the principle of national treatment. In a parallel manner, for countries which are not members of those conventions and which are not deemed to be granting national treatment in the meaning of the Berne Convention, one may expect the worse in terms of copyright infringement. However, a specific reference could be made in the bilateral agreement to a local legislation with the effect of extending protection to the data received by the local ground station. This amounts to a de facto national treatment.

Further, as per the basic concept of copyright protection, it is the expression of the data rather than the idea of the data which is protected. Therefore, under the Berne Convention, it is the enhanced data i.e. the refined and analysed data which is obtained upon analysing the raw data which is being protected. With remote sensing, the unenhanced data is the raw material to which an interpreter applies an idea and, through this process, expresses a protectable, unique creation. It is thus not really the data that is being protected, but rather the analyses and the conclusions resulting from the interpreter's experience and creativity.

Finally, the authors have the right to authorise "the reproduction of their works", but this should not harm their own interest. Quite obviously, the 38 Articles and the appendix of the Berne Convention are mostly geared towards works of the everyday life: remote sensing imagery cannot be protected on the basis of the provisions of this Convention.[42]

The GIS is used to make decisions. The GIS may, for instance, be used to place new roads or power lines, to build subway systems while avoiding the existing underground utilities, to create a school or voting district, or to justify a conservation policy by forecasting an environmental harm from the planned land uses. Occasionally, legal conflicts develop over these decisions. Parents question school district boundaries; landowners dispute

---

41. Excerpts from Article 9, Berne Convention: "(1) Authors of literary and artistic works protected by this Convention shall have the exclusive right of authorizing the reproduction of these works, in any manner or form ... (2) ... provided that such reproduction does not conflict with a normal exploitation of the work and does not unreasonably prejudice the legitimate interests of the author ...." Convention for the Protection of Literary and Artistic Works, 63 U.K.T.S. at 31 (1990); as quoted in infra n. xxiii.

42. Salin, Patrick A., "Proprietary Aspects of Commercial Remote-Sensing Imagery", 13 Nw. J. Int'l L. & Bus. 349 (1992) at http//: international.westlaw.com (last visited Oct 19, 2005).

environmental policies; subway system builders might break the utility lines marked incorrectly on a map generated with the GIS. One or all parties in the conflict might then wish to bring the data or analysis from a GIS into court as evidence in support of a case.

Conclusion

Today, as the use of remote sensing satellite data for both civilian and military purposes is growing, it is also becoming increasingly difficult to distinguish between the military and civilian technologies including remote sensing. In this way, the dual-use technology notion is losing its practical usefulness as it is now depending more on the concrete employment of a specific technology than on its very nature as a typical space activity. Consequently, a clear distinction between the civilian and military technology is becoming more and more difficult to draw.

The observing capability of the remote sensing satellites is increasing and their operation is being privatised rapidly. These developments have given rise to some serious security concerns. The international law entitles all States to freely acquire satellite imagery without the consent of the sensed States. Subject to the applicable principles of international law, a sensing State is entitled to determine the distribution or denial of satellite imagery. The 1986 UN Resolution recognises the right of the sensed State to have access, on a non-discriminatory basis, to the satellite imagery of its own territory. However, contrary to the provisions of this Resolution, several States have started making such access subject to their national security concerns, foreign policy interests or international obligations.

The principle of freedom of exploration and Use of Outer space embodied in the 1967 Treaty and the principle of exclusive jurisdiction in Article 2 (7) of the UN Charter came at stake. In even simpler terms, it was valid to say that if and when remote sensing implied, in practice, taking the high-precision photographs of earth from outer space, the activity was consistent with international law. Conversely, when the data collected was meant to be used—for commercial purposes, for example—a range of issues immediately surfaced. The situation could lead the industrialised countries using modern technology to influence the world markets on the basis of the information obtained and of which the sensed State was unaware. Such was the contention of the developing countries during that decade.

Even though State practice, so far, had included mainly data collection relating to the protection of the environment, the highly sensitive question of national security was ever present. In those days the overriding issue was state sovereignty, which appeared at risk by the advances of science and technology.

Be that as it may, the 1986 Principles did not meet expectations. They were agreed at a time when the commercial sides of this activity were still not envisaged in their full dimension. This is clearly reflected in Principle I, which describes the purpose of remote sensing as improving the natural resources management, land use and the protection of the environment. This approach is strongly reminiscent of the thinking of the previous decade.

Today, most of these Principles reflect the customary international law and, thus, are binding upon States. It is fair to say that they have shed light on the unwritten rules of international law and to some extent have helped to clarify the meaning of some general principles enshrined in the 1967 Space Treaty.

With respect to the status of remote sensing under the International Space Law, it should be noted that the same is a result or consequence of the numerous General Assembly Resolutions and recommendations that are bestowed with a mere advisory nature not having a legislative or quasi-legislative authority.

5.   On Drafting a Viable Model of National Space Legislation for India

SANDEEPA BHAT B.

Introduction

With the beginning of the space era in the second half of the twentieth century, one of the significant questions that cropped up was the legal regulation of the space activities. The United Nations took a requisite initiative to develop the space law at an international level. This resulted in the initial development of nonbinding soft laws[1] and the subsequent conceptualisation of binding hard laws[2] to govern the outer space activities. Unfortunately, the development of hard laws at the international level had a setback with the failure of the Moon Agreement in 1979.[3] It is reflected in the fact that no international treaty on outer space was entered into after 1979 due to the absence of a consensus among the States. At present, apart from a select few customary norms, the outer space activities are primarily governed at the international level by five space treaties entered into in the 1960s and 70s.

It is crucial to note here that space activities during the 1960s and 70s were confined to State-oriented activities and therefore, the five space treaties exclusively deal with the regulation of State activities in outer space. However, during the last more than four decades, space activities have transformed significantly with the changing technology. Space investments have moved from public sector to private sector with the knowledge of manifold commercial uses of outer space. This shift has necessitated separate

---

1. In the form of UN General Assembly resolutions.
2. The binding norms are in the form of five major space treaties, which are: Treaty on Principles Governing the Activities of States in the Exploration and Use of Outer Space, including the Moon and Other Celestial Bodies (Outer Space Treaty) 1967; Agreement on the Rescue of Astronauts, the Return of Astronauts and the Return of Objects Launched into Outer Space (Rescue Agreement) 1968; Convention on International Liability for Damage Caused by Space Objects (Liability Convention) 1972; Convention on Registration of Objects Launched into Outer Space (Registration Convention) 1975 and the Agreement Governing the Activities of States on the Moon and Other Celestial Bodies (Moon Agreement) 1979.
3. Only 16 States have ratified the Moon Agreement till today. See "Status of International Agreements Relating to Activities in Outer Space as at 1 January 2015", UNCOPUOS Doc. A/AC.105/C.2/2015/CRP.8 (08 April 2015).

norms to regulate the ever-increasing private space activities, which have not been covered under the international norms.

Since a State consensus at the international level is not forthcoming, enacting a national space legislation to fill in the existing more than four decades of the void in law is the only available option for the States. In light of this, an attempt has been made here to analyse the major prerequisites in the national space legislation for India, which is presently being attempted by the Indian Space Research Organisation (ISRO).[4]

Before delving in detail into the essential elements of the Indian national space legislation, it is important to note that the primary objective of a national space legislation for India shall be to regulate and also to promote the private space activities. Regulation is absolutely required for an orderly development in the sphere of outer space. It is undeniable; especially in the light of the experiences that we have got from the civil aviation crisis in India.[5] However, we should also keep in mind that the regulation should not be excessive, since it may have a chilling effect on the private space investments in India. Hence, a delicate balance between the regulation and promotion of private space activities has to be struck in the national space legislation. Added to this, the Indian national space legislation should be in compliance with India's international obligations under the Outer Space Treaty, Rescue Agreement, Liability Convention and Registration Convention to which India is a party. In this backdrop, the Indian national space legislation shall primarily address the issues of licensing and supervision of the private space activities, the registration of launches and the liability for damage caused, among other significant aspects.

Licensing and Supervision of Private Space Activities
Every space activity, whether public or private, shall be subject to license and continued supervision by the 'appropriate state' under Article VI of

4. In January 2015, the first round of a workshop was held at the ISRO Headquarters, Bangalore in this direction. See <http://pib.nic.in/newsite/PrintRelease.aspx?relid=123526> Last visited, 15 August 2015. This effort has been supplemented by the round table conference held at the National Law School of India University, Bangalore, during July 2015. See <http://newspaceindia.com/excerpts-of-round-table-conference-on-issues-for-national-space-legislation/> Last visited, 15 August 2015.

5. See M. G. Arun, "Heartburn in the Air", available at <http://indiatoday.intoday.in/story/spicejet-crisis-indias-civil-aviation-sector-kalanidhi-maran/1/414917.html> Last visited, 15 August 2015. See also Tony Tyler, "Aviation Crisis: Common Vision to Help Fix Problems like High Taxes, Investment Curbs", available at <http://articles.economictimes.indiatimes.com/2012-05-31/news/31922058_1_tax-on-air-tickets-aviation-service-tax> Last visited, 15 August 2015.

the Outer Space Treaty.[6] This necessitates the establishment of a licensing authority in India along with detailed norms on the grant, renewal and revocation of licences for private space activities. The licensing procedure should include a demonstration of technical capability by the private space operator.[7] The requirement of a minimum insurance coverage to discharge the liability in case of an accident has to be mandated under the national space legislation. Compliance with the public safety standards and a respect of the national security interests need to be specifically reflected in the legislation. The norm on continued supervision requires the mechanism to be set at the domestic level for inspection by the appropriate authority and submission of periodic reports by the private players. Since the space activities involve high technology, which the operators desire to keep confidential, the inspection procedure should be developed in such a manner that the clandestine activities get checked without any breach of the technological confidentiality. Supplementing these provisions, the national space legislation should prescribe punishments for the violations of norms in the course of private space activities. All these are very significant, since the failure of the State to comply with these requirements results in the attaching of international responsibility to the State.[8]

One of the significant issues that have not been addressed under the space treaties is the transferability of the licences granted pursuant to Article VI of the Outer Space Treaty. This is of tremendous significance in the modern-day private space activities, wherein the sales of space assets are quite common. A sale of space assets cannot be implemented unless the licenses can be transferred to the purchasers, since the purchaser cannot carry on space activities without an appropriate licence.[9] The saleability of satellites is a matter of tremendous importance to the private space investor,

---

6. As per Article VI, "States Parties to the Treaty shall bear international responsibility for national activities in outer space, including the Moon and other celestial bodies, whether such activities are carried on by governmental agencies or by non-governmental entities, and for assuring that national activities are carried out in conformity with the provisions set forth in the present Treaty. The activities of non-governmental entities in outer space, including the Moon and other celestial bodies, shall require authorization and continuing supervision by the appropriate State Party to the Treaty."

7. This is very significant as every State is responsible for the activities of its private players under Article VI of the Outer Space Treaty.

8. Julian Hermida, *Legal Basis for a National Space Legislation* (New York: Kluwer Academic Publishers, 2004) pp. 7 & 8.

9. F. G . von der Dunk, "The Origins of Authorization: Article VI of the Outer Space Treaty and International Space Law" in Frans G. von der Dunk (ed.), *National Space Legislation in Europe* (Leiden: Martinus Nijhoff, 2011) pp. 3-28.

as the investor may resort to a sale in the case of recurring losses and thereby, get back at least a portion of his investments. In the absence of a transfer of licence, the investors may find it difficult to bear the risk of complete loss. This would shake the confidence of the investors in space investments. Therefore, the national space legislation should provide the mechanism for a transfer of licences in case of sale of space objects.[10]

Registration of Space Objects

The Indian national space legislation needs to incorporate the procedure for the registration of space objects as required under the Registration Convention. The existing national registry of space objects has to register the space objects of private players in India;[11] for which, an appropriate procedure has to be laid down. In addition, the mechanism has to be developed for the transmission of information to the Secretary-General of the United Nations towards international registration.[12] An arrangement should be made for the transmission of any additional information to the Secretary-General about the space objects from time to time.[13] For all these purposes, a single window has to be established along with the mechanism to test the veracity of the information intended to be transmitted.

Another crucial question that remains to be addressed is the possibility of change in the 'State of registry'.[14] This question has remained unaddressed under the international space treaties, and there are two groups of scholars advocating two opposite arguments. On the one hand, it is argued that the space treaties do not provide for a transfer of the State of registry and

---

10. "Draft Report of the Working Group on National Legislation Relevant to the Peaceful Exploration and Use of Outer Space", UNCOPUS Doc. A/AC.105/C.2/2011/CRP.4 (24 March 2011) p. 11.
11. As per Article II of the Registration Convention, which states: "When a space object is launched into earth orbit or beyond, the launching State shall register the space object by means of an entry in an appropriate registry which it shall maintain."
12. As per Articles III & IV of the Registration Convention. While Article III mandates the international registration, Article IV enlists the information to be provided to the UN Secretary-General in connection with the international registration.
13. This would be in furtherance of Article IV (2) of the Registration Convention, which states: "Each State of registry may, from time to time, provide the Secretary-General of the United Nations with additional information concerning a space object carried on its registry."
14. 'State of registry' is defined under Article I (c) of the Registration Convention as "The term "State of registry" means a launching State on whose registry a space object is carried in accordance with article II."

therefore, registration cannot be transferred.[15] On the other hand, it is contended that the space treaties do not explicitly prohibit such a transfer and therefore, a transfer of the State of registry is permissible.[16] However, with the increased private space activities, it has become necessary to find a way for the transfer of the State of registry, especially in case of the sale of space objects from one State to another. This is because the registration of the space object by a State results in several consequences under the space treaties. The obligation to retain jurisdiction and control on the space objects and the personnel thereof,[17] the right to receive the astronauts and space objects in case of emergency landing,[18] the liability to pay compensation for the damage caused by space activities,[19] the application of municipal laws to deal with the activities of astronauts and personnel in outer space,[20] etc. are some of the significant consequences of the registration of space objects. In light of these consequences, the national space legislation needs to incorporate a mandatory transfer of the State of registry as a prerequisite for the sale of space objects to other states, in the absence of which, India would be in violation of its international commitments under the space treaties.[21]

---

15. Kai-Uwe Schrogl and Julian Hermida, 'Change of Ownership, Change of Registry? Which Objects to Register, What Data to be Furnished, When, and Until When?', *Proceedings of Forty-Sixth Colloquium on Law of Outer Space*, 2004, pp. 454 - 463 at pp. 457 & 458.

16. Ibid.

17. As per Article VIII of the Outer Space Treaty, "A State Party to the Treaty on whose registry an object launched into outer space is carried shall retain jurisdiction and control over such object, and over any personnel thereof, while in outer space or on a celestial body."

18. As per Article V of the Outer Space Treaty, "States Parties to the Treaty shall regard astronauts as envoys of mankind in outer space and shall render to them all possible assistance in the event of accident, distress, or emergency landing on the territory of another State Party or on the high seas. When astronauts make such a landing, they shall be safely and promptly returned to the State of registry of their space vehicle."

19. Though the liability to pay compensation is on the launching State/s, the State of registry, being a launching State would be easily identified by the victim State. Therefore, there is every possibility of the victim State proceeding against the State of registry under the principle of joint and several liabilities enshrined under the Liability Convention.

20. Since we are not having any readily available law to deal with any tort, crime or infringement of the intellectual property rights in outer space, the application of the State of registry's law is argued by the scholars to be a preferred solution. See generally Julian Hermida, "Criminal and Intellectual Property Jurisdiction in the International Space Station" in Sandeepa Bhat B. (ed.), *Outer Space Law: From Theory to Practice*, (Hyderabad: ICFAI University Press, 2009) pp. 169-188.

21. This would primarily include the violation of the licensing and supervision clause as well as the jurisdiction and control clause under Articles VI and VIII of the Outer Space Treaty respectively.

Liability for the Damage Caused

Article VII of the Outer Space Treaty,[22] supplemented by the Liability Convention,[23] provides a detailed regime of the international liability of the launching States for the damage caused by the space activities. The launching State's liability under the space treaties extends to private space activities. Scholars are divided in their opinion as to the imposition of such liability on States. Some scholars are of the view that such an imposition of liability is unintentional, since the drafters of the Outer Space Treaty and the Liability Convention did not foresee the private space activities. As the drafters were only considering the regulation of State activities in outer space, the space treaties mention only about State liability.[24] However, the other group of scholars advocates that the imposition of liability on the State for its private players' space activities is intentional. This is because of the enormous risk involved in the space activities, which may result in catastrophic damage and eventual bankruptcy of the private player involved. In such a situation, the victim shall not be deprived of relief simply due to the inability of the space player to pay compensation.[25]

Whatever may be the argument on State liability for private space activities, the States are keen to shift the burden of liability arising out of increasing private space activities.[26] But, the crucial question in this

---

22. "Each State Party to the Treaty that launches or procures the launching of an object into outer space, including the Moon and other celestial bodies, and each State Party from whose territory or facility an object is launched, is internationally liable for damage to another State Party to the Treaty or to its natural or juridical persons by such object or its component parts on the Earth, in air space or in outer space, including the Moon and other celestial bodies."

23. As per Article II, "A launching State shall be absolutely liable to pay compensation for damage caused by its space object on the surface of the earth or to aircraft flight." As per Article III, "In the event of damage being caused elsewhere than on the surface of the earth to a space object of one launching State or to persons or property on board such a space object by a space object of another launching State, the latter shall be liable only if the damage is due to its fault or the fault of persons for whom it is responsible." These provisions are supplemented by the remaining provisions of the Liability Convention.

24. This view is reflected in the writings of Henri Wassenbergh when he argues that the liability of the launching State/s shall be restricted to the governmental space activities. Henri A. Wassenbergh, *Principles of Outer Space Law in Hindsight* (Dordrecht: Kluwer Academic Publishers, 1991) p. 29.

25. John M. Kelson, "State Responsibility and the Abnormally Dangerous Activity", *Harvard International Law Journal,* Vol. 13, 1972, pp. 197-244 at p. 216.

26. Ricky J. Lee, "The Convention on International Liability for Damage Caused by Space Objects and the Domestic Regulatory Responses to its Implications", p. 1, available at <http://www.unoosa.org/pdf/sap/2003/repkorea/presentations/lee.pdf> Last visited, 15 August 2015.

regard is: how to shift the liability with minimum damage to both the public and private interest without violating the international obligations? Insurance coverage or demonstration of financial responsibility is the primary mechanism used in most of the jurisdictions to cover the first stage of compensation.[27] Any claim in excess of the insurance coverage or the financial responsibility of the private player is discharged by adopting different systems across the globe. To quote few examples, the United States adopts a limited governmental liability,[28] Australia adopts burden shifting to private players[29] and the United Kingdom adopts the government payment and subsequent private player indemnification models.[30]

Neither the United States' limited liability model nor the Australian burden-shifting model is in conformity with the norms of space treaties, since they explicitly mention the 'unlimited liability' of the 'launching State/s'. Though the United Kingdom's model of government shouldering the liability and seeking indemnification from private players is in compliance with the space treaties, it would be difficult for India to implement such a model in its national space legislation. This is due to the drastic difference in the economic situations prevailing in a developed State like the United Kingdom and a developing State like India. Therefore, a suitable model for shouldering the liability has to be adopted in the Indian national space legislation. One such model that comes to the mind of the author is the nuclear liability fund created in the United States to shoulder the liability arising out of nuclear damage,[31] which has also been tried to be adopted in

---

27. Ibid., pp. 21-24.
28. As per 51 U.S. Code § 50915 (a), the United States' government is liable to pay compensation over and above the liability insurance, but subject to a limit of $ 1,500,000,000 (plus additional amounts necessary to reflect inflation occurring after January 1, 1989).
29. Sections 67 & 68 of the Space Activities Act 1998 (Australia) clearly mention the liability of 'responsible party', and Section 8 of the Act defines the 'responsible party' as the private player involved in the concerned space activity. See also supra note 26, p. 18.
30. Sec. 10 (1) of the Outer Space Act 1986 (UK) states: "A person to whom this Act applies shall indemnify Her Majesty's government in the United Kingdom against any claims brought against the government in respect of damage or loss arising out of activities carried on by him to which this Act applies."
31. This fund created by the contribution of nuclear operators under the Price–Anderson Act 1957 is known as the Price–Anderson Fund. See Elizabeth J. Wilson and Sara Bergan, "Managing Liability: Comparing Radioactive Waste Disposal and Carbon Dioxide Storage in Frence L. Toth (ed.), *Geological Disposal of Carbon Dioxide and Radioactive Waste: A Comparative Assessment* (Dordrecht: Springer, 2011) pp. 263-294 at p. 279.

India under the Civil Liability for the Nuclear Damage Act 2010.[32] Such a pool may be created by the regular contribution of private players out of the profits generated by their space activities. This would avoid an unnecessary burden on the public funds arising out of the private space activities in India. At the same time, the creation of a pool of funds would relieve the private space actors from the tension of bankruptcy in the case of accidents.

Another issue to be dealt with under the national space legislation is the status of the liability for the damage caused after the sale of the space objects to foreign players. As per the space treaties, the liability for damage would always be with the launching State/s. But if the damage has been caused to a third party after the sale of a space object from a launching State to a State that is not connected to the launch, holding the launching State still liable does not seem to be in compliance with the principles of justice and equity.[33] Hence, the national space legislation shall address this issue by mandating the shifting of international liability from the launching State to the State to which the purchaser of the space object belongs. In the absence of a such transfer of liability, the very sale of space objects shall not be permitted to prevent the possibility of any future unexpected liability.

Other Significant Aspects

In addition to the detailed mechanisms on the above three issues, there is a requirement of incorporating provisions on the other significant aspects of current concern in the national space legislation. To start with, a prohibition on the claim of celestial property rights is an absolute necessity under the national space legislation for India. Recent trends in different parts of the world depict a dangerous trend of claiming celestial property rights on frivolous grounds.[34] Such trends have gone to the extent of starting the business of selling parts of the moon and other celestial bodies.[35] Though these activities are in violation of Article II of the Outer Space Treaty, the

---

32. Section 7 (2) of the Act states; "For the purpose of meeting part of its liability under clause (a) or clause (c) of sub-section (1), the Central Government may establish a fund to be called the Nuclear Liability Fund by charging such amount of levy from the operators, in such manner, as may be prescribed."

33. One of the basic tenets of justice and equity is that one who reaps the benefit should also incur the burden. Going by this, imposing the liability on the launching State, which is nowhere connected with the space activity after the sale of space object, is against the sound principles of justice and equity.

34. See Adam Mann, "Space Cases: The Weirdest Legal Claims in Outer Space", available at <http://www.wired.com/2012/06/space-cases/> Last visited, 15 August 2015.

35. See <www.lunarembassy.com> Last visited, 15 August 2015.

claimants have tried to justify their claims on the contention that Article II of the Outer Space Treaty prohibits only the national appropriation but not the claim of private property rights by the individuals.[36] The Board of Directors of the International Institute of Space Law[37] and many space law scholars[38] have highlighted the requirement of taking appropriate actions under the municipal laws to prevent such fraudulent activities. It is also argued that under Article VI of the Outer Space Treaty, 'appropriate State' has the responsibility to prevent such private space activities.[39] The Law of the Russian Federation is one of the classic examples of bringing into force the prohibition on celestial property rights.[40] In the light of these, the national space legislation for India needs to incorporate a provision for prohibiting any celestial property claims.

36. Ibid. See also Alan Wasser and Douglas Jobes, "Space Settlements, Property Rights, and International Law: Could a Lunar Settlement Claim the Lunar Real Estate it Needs to Survive?", *Journal of Air Law and Commerce*, Vol. 73, 2008, pp. 37-73 at pp. 49 & 50.

37. The statement issued by the Board of Directors of IISL in 2004 states: "Article VI of the Outer Space Treaty provides that "States bear international responsibility for national activities in outer space, including the Moon and other celestial bodies, whether such activities are carried on by governmental agencies or by non-governmental entities", that is, private parties, and "for assuring that national activities are carried out in conformity with the provisions set forth in the present Treaty". Article VI further provides that "the activities of nongovernmental entities in outer space, including the Moon and other celestial bodies, shall require authorization and continuing supervision by the appropriate State Party to the Treaty. ... According to international law, States party to a treaty are under a duty to implement the terms of that treaty within their national legal systems. Therefore, to comply with their obligations under Articles II and VI of the Outer Space Treaty, States Parties are under a duty to ensure that, in their legal systems, transactions regarding claims to property rights to the Moon and other celestial bodies or parts thereof, have no legal significance or recognized legal effect." See "Statement by the Board of Directors of the International Institute of Space Law (IISL) on Claims to Property Rights Regarding the Moon and Other Celestial Bodies", available at <http://www.iislweb.org/docs/IISL_Outer_Space_Treaty_Statement.pdf> Last visited, 15 August 2015.

38. See for example, Virgiliu Pop, *Who Owns the Moon?* (Springer, 2008) p. 18; See also Johanna Catena, "Legal Matters Relating to the "Settlement" of "Outposts" on the Moon", *Proceedings of Forty-Seventh Colloquium on Law of the Outer Space*, 2005, pp. 414-424 at p. 422.

39. See supra note 37. Frans von der Dunk, while commenting on the sale of celestial bodies by Dennis Hope, states that "...under international law the U.S. government should unequivocally make clear that these practices are not based on any sound legal premise." See Robert Roy Britt, "Lunar Land Grab: Celestial Real Estate Sales Soar", available at <http://www.rense.com/general48/sour.htm > Last visited, 15 August 2015.

40. As per Section 17 (5) of the Law of the Russian Federation about Space Activity, "The rights of jurisdiction and control over space objects, as well as of ownership thereof shall not affect the legal status of the area of outer space or the surface or subsoil of a celestial body occupied by it."

A prohibition on military activities by the private players shall be the next significant provision to be incorporated under the national space legislation. Under Article IV of the Outer Space Treaty, we find a prohibition on the placement of nuclear weapons and any other kind of weapons of mass destruction in outer space. There is also a mandate to use the celestial bodies for peaceful purposes.[41] However, the provision suffers from several loopholes due to drafting errors. One of the major loopholes is the absence of prohibition on all kind of weapons as well as all types of military activities in outer space.[42] The national space legislation should strengthen the norms of demilitarisation by prohibiting any type of military activity in the outer space by the private players. This would be essential to prevent the escalation of terror and the breach of peace in the course of maintaining international peace and security.

The protection of the outer space environment in the course of private space activities also needs a special mention in the national space legislation, since our future in space is completely dependent on keeping the outer space environment away from pollution. A provision needs to be incorporated to implement the mandate of Article IX of the Outer Space Treaty, which prohibits a harmful contamination of outer space and adverse changes in the earth's environment in the course of outer space activities.[43] In this process, a mandatory scheme for an environmental impact assessment of every space project is required. Added to this, the law must impose liability on the private players to pay damages for any damage caused by space ventures. This would on the one hand act as a deterrent against the carrying on of space activities in an unregulated manner, and on the other hand, provide funds for reinstating the outer space environment.

---

41. Article IV of the Outer Space Treaty states: "States Parties to the Treaty undertake not to place in orbit around the Earth any objects carrying nuclear weapons or any other kinds of weapons of mass destruction, install such weapons on celestial bodies, or station such weapons in outer space in any other manner. The Moon and other celestial bodies shall be used by all States Parties to the Treaty exclusively for peaceful purposes."

42. "Existing International Legal Instruments and Prevention of the Weaponization of Outer Space", A Non-Paper by Chinese and Russian Delegations to the Conference on Disarmament, 26 August 2004, available at <http://www.nuclearfiles.org/menu/key-issues/space-weapons/issues/reachingcriticalwill_PAROS2.pdf> Last visited, 16 August 2015.

43. Article IX states: "States Parties to the Treaty shall pursue studies of outer space, including the Moon and other celestial bodies, and conduct exploration of them so as to avoid their harmful contamination and also adverse changes in the environment of the Earth resulting from the introduction of extraterrestrial matter and, where necessary, shall adopt appropriate measures for this purpose."

The provision to deal with the space tourism is the next significant aspect to be incorporated in the national space legislation of India. Though India has not witnessed any space tourism activity till date, it is going to start in the near future. Once the space tourism activities begin, several legal challenges would come to the forefront.[44] The use of aerospace vehicles for space tourism would pose a difficulty of choice between the aviation law and space law for application to the various aspects of space tourism including registration, licensing, continued supervision, liability, jurisdiction, control, etc.[45] The status of space tourists in the case of emergency landing needs clarification, since the space treaties speak only about the emergency assistance to astronauts and the personnel of space objects.[46]

Patent protection in outer space is yet another area to be addressed in the national space legislation of India. With the establishment of the International Space Station[47] and the development of plans to establish stations on the moon and other celestial bodies, space research is going to be the next big event in space exploration. However, we are not having any universal patent law that can be made applicable in the outer space to deal with the granting of patents or combating the infringement of earthly patents in outer space.[48] This leaves the States to apply the municipal patent law extra-territorially on the basis of the connecting factors to deal with the space inventions or infringements. The United States has already done such an application through Section 105 of the Patent Act.[49]

44. See generally, Paulina E. Sikorska, "The Mission (Im)possible: Towards a Comprehensive Legal Framework Regulating Safety Issues of Point to Point Suborbital Flights", *Jurisprudence*, Vol. 21, No. 4, 2014, pp. 1055-1078.

45. See generally, Stephan Hobe, "Legal Aspects of Space Tourism", *Nebraska Law Review,* Vol. 86, Issue 2, 2007, pp. 439-458.

46. Yanal Abul Failat, "Space Tourism: A Synopsis on its Legal Challenges", *Irish Law Journal*, Vol. 1, 2012, pp. 120-151 at pp. 125 & 126.

47. The International Space Station is a joint endeavour of the United States, Russia, Canada, Japan and the European Space Agency.

48. Sandeepa Bhat B., "Inventions in Outer Space: Need for Reconsideration of the Patent Regime", *Journal of Space Law*, Vol. 36, No. 1, 2010, pp. 1-17 at pp. 6 & 10.

49. 35 U.S. Code § 105 states: "Any invention made, used or sold in outer space on a space object or component thereof under the jurisdiction or control of the United States shall be considered to be made, used or sold within the United States for the purposes of this title, except with respect to any space object or component thereof that is specifically identified and otherwise provided for by an international agreement to which the United States is a party, or with respect to any space object or component thereof that is carried on the registry of a foreign state in accordance with the Convention on Registration of Objects Launched into Outer Space."

Norms on private space financing and investments is another aspect that may find its way to the national space legislation of India. This is especially required in the light of the failure to unify the space financing laws under the UNIDROIT system.[50] In the absence of a suitable regime to govern the rights and duties of the creditors and debtors, it is difficult to win the confidence of the creditors to invest in risky space ventures.[51] Therefore, a sustained growth in private space investments can be achieved only by clarifying the space financing laws.

It is also desirable to have a separate dispute settlement mechanism for dealing with the disputes arising out of liability to compensate for the damage caused by space activities. This has been found as essential due to the problems in locating the court of the appropriate jurisdiction in case of a damage caused in multiple territories subject to the jurisdiction of different courts. Though such a case may be brought before the Supreme Court, given the work pressure of the Supreme Court, one cannot expect a speedy disposal of the space liability disputes. Added to this, the ordinary courts of law may also find a difficulty in the lack of expertise in dealing with liability arising out of space activities. Therefore, a dispute settlement mechanism to provide a speedy justice to the victims of space disasters would be useful. An analogy for this purpose can be drawn from the mechanism developed under the Indian nuclear liability regime.[52]

Finally, the national space legislation of India has to prescribe punishments for the violation of different provisions under the enactment. The punishments may range from payment of compensation or penalty to the cancellation of licences of the private players.

Concluding Remarks

In the wake of the huge potentiality of private space investments in India, the requirement of a national space legislation for India is an absolute

---

50. UNIDROIT has attempted to unify the space financing laws by adopting a two-tier system consisting of (a) Convention on International Interests in Mobile Equipment (Cape Town Convention) 2001 and (b) Protocol to the Convention on International Interests in Mobile Equipment on Matters Specific to Space Assets (Space Protocol) 2012. However, the system has not come into force due to the failure of the Space Protocol to acquire the required number of ratifications. See <http://www.unidroit.org/status-2012-space> 16 August 2015.

51. Mark J. Sundahl, *The Cape Town Convention: Its Application to Space Assets and Relation to Law of Outer Space* (Leiden: Brill, 2013) pp. 7-14.

52. See Civil Liability for Nuclear Damage Act 2010, Chapters III, IV & V.

necessity. Clarification in the law is not only required from the perspective of the State but also from the private players' perspective. This is because the clarity in law helps them in taking the necessary measures to deal with the requirements. One such example is the clarification of the private space actor's liability, which helps the private player to shoulder the burden by procuring the necessary liability insurance or by other mechanisms. Understandably, it might not be possible to comprehensively cover everything in one national space legislation. However, this issue can be taken care of by requisite elaborations through the supplementary rules to be provided from time to time.

The initiative taken by the ISRO in drafting the national space legislation for India is timely and commendable. However, the author is of the strong opinion that the drafting of a national space legislation has to be done by persons with a legal background and not by those with a scientific background. Of course, the legal experts need assistance of the scientific community in drafting the national space legislation in a high-technology field like that of outer space activities. Drafting of the legal provisions requires an utmost care and specialised skill, since any failure to use the appropriate words would result in absurdity. There is a narrow line of distinction between the interpretation and misinterpretation of laws. It is obvious that the miscreants would do their best to evade the law through misinterpretations and therefore, it is a challenge for the lawmakers to strengthen the four corners of law to overcome the problem of evasion. In the absence of such a crafty drafting, a law would be more of a menace than being of any use. Therefore, it is our duty to see to it that we are not setting a bad precedent in terms of space lawmaking.

6. State Practices Towards National Space Legislation*

KUMAR ABHIJEET

Introduction

There is no doubt that India has had a robust and responsible history and a promising future in the exploration and use of outer space. The National Space Legislation is a giant step in the direction of preserving and continuing the legacy of our heritage. Most of the spacefaring nations have adopted their respective national space legislations and the study of their respective legislation further contributes to my perplexity—which model is suitable for India? Are there any lessons to be learned from the existing national space legislations of the various spacefaring countries? To answer this, let me go back to the discourse—why a national space legislation should be there for India. The obvious reason is the increasing commercialisation and privatisation of the space activities in the light of international obligations. The general issues in the drafting of a national space legislation[1] include defining the scope and applicability, liability,[2] authorisation,[3] supervision,[4] registration,[5] indemnification,[6] environment considerations,[7] etc. In the light of these issues, the paper tries to reveal the practices of the various spacefaring nations.

---

*   This paper is revised form of the paper presented at the ISRO workshop (16th -17th January, 2015) on National Space Act.

1.   See the UNGA (68/74 of 2013) Resolution on Recommendations on Enhancing the Practice of States and International Intergovernmental Organizations in Registering Space Objects.

2   See Article VII, Stephan Hobe/ Bernhard Schmidt-Tedd/ Kai-Uwe Schrogl (eds.) *Cologne Commentary on Space Law*, Volume 1, pp.103-126, Carl Heymanns Verlag 2009.

3.   See Article VI, Stephan Hobe/ Bernhard Schmidt-Tedd/ Kai-Uwe Schrogl (eds.) *Cologne Commentary on Space Law*, Volume 1, pp.126-145, Carl Heymanns Verlag 2009.

4.   Ibid.

5.   See Article VIII, Stephan Hobe/ Bernhard Schmidt-Tedd/ Kai-Uwe Schrogl (eds.) *Cologne Commentary on Outer Space Law*, Volume 1, pp.146-168, Carl Heymanns Verlag 2009.

6.   Michael Gerhard, "Potential "Building Blocks" of a National Space Legislation in the Proceedings of the Project 2001: Workshop on National Space Legislation", Munich, 5/6 December 2000, p.183.

7.   See Article IX, Stephan Hobe/ Bernhard Schmidt-Tedd/ Kai-Uwe Schrogl (eds.) *Cologne Commentary on Outer Space Law*, Volume 1, pp.169-182, Carl Heymanns Verlag 2009.

The Issue of Delimitation

Currently, space activities are being majorly carried out by the Government of India or precisely, the ISRO. The Antrix Corp. has been doing an excellent job of commercialising our space services. We have repeatedly demonstrated our capability in the launch services. The GSLV and PSLV, indigenously developed with a self-reliant technology, are attracting global customers from all over the world. The GSLV MK III is on way and with its operationalisation, we are going to be the pioneers in the launch service sector as envisioned by our Prime Minister.[8] Certainly, it is a matter of pride for us but as a space lawyer I vision it as being an unlimited liability.

Article VII OST—"*Each State Party to the treaty that launches or procures the a lunching of an object into Outer Space . . . and each State Party from whose territory or facility an object is launched is internationally liable for damage to another State party . . .*"

The above international obligation clearly manifests that when India launches or when a launch is be undertaken from Sriharikota[9] or India's facility is being offered for launch, India shall be liable for the damage caused by the object launched from these facilities or launching centres. The next issue is how do we determine the liability. No deep space exploration is needed to answer it because the Liability Convention is clear on this issue that the liability for the damage caused in outer space is determined on a fault basis[10] and for the damages caused in air space or on Earth it is an absolute liability.[11] But, the question is, where is the boundary line between air space and outer space? Many theories have been put forward in this regard but the international community has not reached any common agreement on this point. Since the issue of delimitation remains unresolved, how is India going to discharge its liability for any damage being caused, knowing the fact that space vehicles travel through airspace first and then into the outer space? The progress of sub-orbital flights is further aggravating the cause of delimitation of air space. Our national space legislation certainly cannot wait till the international

---

8. See the text of the speech of PM Narendra Modi on the PSLV-C23 launch at Sriharikota, June 30th 2014, available at http://www.narendramodi.in/text-speech-of-pm-narendra-modi-at-pslv-c23-launch-at-sriharikota.
9. The space port of India
10. See Article III (Fault Liability), Stephan Hobe/ Bernhard Schmidt-Tedd/ Kai-Uwe Schrogl (eds.) *Cologne Commentary on Space Law*, Volume II, pp. 131-136, Carl Heymanns Verlag 2013.
11. See Article II (Absolute Liability), Stephan Hobe/ Bernhard Schmidt-Tedd/ Kai-Uwe Schrogl (eds.) *Cologne Commentary on Space Law*, Volume II, pp.116-130, Carl Heymanns Verlag 2013.

community resolves it; but shall we, like other nations, make it dependent on the sands of time? No national space legislation except for Australia's,[12] has attempted to answer this question by limiting the airspace up to 100 km. Will the National Space Act of India give space to the issue of delimitation?

Issue of Liability

Article VII of the OST is a 'Pandora's box' which has placed unlimited liability on the launching state. Pioneering authors have profusely written that a 'procurement of launch' is not limited to having an actual control over the launch; rather, it includes wherever there is a possibility for control.[13] This is rather an alarming concern because India is aspiring to commercialise its launch services and open the doors to private participants and foreign customers. All space objects which have been launched by India either for itself or for others till date and the future space objects to be launched by India either for itself or for others exposes India to an unlimited liability because the damage caused by a space object is primarily imputed to the launching state which has often been titled as "once a launching state forever a launching state".[14] Some States like the Netherlands have used their national space legislation[15] as a tool to escape from their liability by virtue of procurement. They do not consider the liability arising from procurement of space activity by private participants as their national liability. Should India also have a limited scope to determine its liability or shall it go for a progressive legislation? Having an escapist tendency is no solution, rather it is an invitation to the problem contingent on the time factor. Limiting liability makes work at the domestic level but not at the international level.

Conditions of Authorisation and Supervision

Since India aspires for a commercial usage of space wherein the necessity of the private sector has been realised due to its increasing competency both

---

12. See Space Activities Act 1998, available at http://www.unoosa.org/oosa/en/SpaceLaw/national/state-index.html

13. Michael Gerhard, "The State of the Art and Recent Trends in the Development of National Space Law" in Christian Brunner and Edith Walter (eds.) *National Space Law: Development in Europe: Challenges for Small Countries*, Bohlau Verlag, 2008, p.68.

14. Frans G. von der Dunk, "The International Law of Outer Space and Consequences at the National Level for India: Towards an Indian National Space Law?" in *Indian Yearbook of International Law and Policy* (2009).

15. See Rules Concerning Space Activities and the Establishment of a Registry of Space Objects (Space Activities Act) 2008.

technologically and financially, the international obligation demands to authorise and supervise their activity. How do we authorise their activity? State practices suggest that it has been achieved through licensing by imposing conditions of compliance. What should be the conditions for licensing them? State practices suggest that national security, safety and international obligation are the prime considerations for granting license.

Besides these, the States have also given due importance to technical and financial conditions of the licensee, environmental safeguards, etc. Supervision of authorised space activities ensures that the activities are under a constant vigilance of the Government and the risk of damage being caused is minimised. With regard to the supervision of space activities, a universality of practice has been seen among the states. Most of the states seek the furnishing of information, documents and an access to the premises where the authorised space activities are being undertaken. The powers of seizure and search have been conferred on the authorised officers should the necessity demand.

Insurance and Indemnification

Thus, commercial launches and launches on behalf of private participants demand some financial surety to be reimbursed in case India is to pay for any of the liabilities arising. The State practice suggests that generally the operator is under an obligation to take a compulsory insurance depending upon the risk involved. Should the State be made liable for the damages caused by authorised space activities, the respective State reserves the right to seek indemnification to the extent the damage has been paid. While taking insurance, care is to be taken that the insurance condition does not become an excessive burden on the operators so much so that they get discouraged from participating in space activities. State practices suggest that States have taken a balanced approach towards the safeguarding of national interests as well as for facilitating the private participants. Currently, the UK[16] has made an unlimited liability on the operators for damages caused by their authorised activities but the Government is planning to put a limit[17]

---

16. UK Outer Space Act 1986.
17. See "Reform of the Outer Space Act 1986: Summary of Responses and Government Response to Consultation", UKSA/13/1326. "In the majority of cases, involving missions employing established launchers, satellite platforms and operational profiles, this insurance cover would be limited to 60 million euro. For each license application, a risk assessment will be performed to consider the potential risks posed by the mission and a commensurate level of insurance cover will be determined. The Government will retain the flexibility to increase the liability cap/insurance requirement for any non-standard high risk mission."

on this liability as has been done under the French Space Act.[18] The French Government has limited the liability of the authorised space operator to the extent of the insurance amount. However, in order to avail this privilege the operator must come with clean hands i.e. there should not be any wilful misconduct on behalf of the operator.

Limited liability is also experienced in the Belgium Space Act[19] but the liability is determined on the basis of the average turnover. The maximum liability for only the authorised operator has been limited to a ten percent of the average turnover generated by the operator over the three years preceding the year in which the authorisation request was submitted.[20] Where it is not possible to ascertain an average turnover for three years, calculation is based on the financial years which have ended and the projection for future financial years. This has been done so that the basis of calculating the liability remains three consecutive years.[21] Thus, there is no fixed amount, but it is dependent on the turnover of the operator. The greater the turnover, the greater would be the liability of the operator.

The Austrian Space Legislation[22] is more progressive towards the facilitating of private participants. In order to cover damages caused to third parties, an operator has an obligation to take out an insurance covering not less than 60 000 000 euro per insurance claim. The amount of insurance may be reduced for the operators undertaking space activities in public interest if they serve science, research and education. This is a very, very broad category of liability exclusion. Though, it may be a boost to the private participant, on the other hand, an enormous liability would be recurring on the Government.

But, this liability could be avoided by diligent supervision.

Transfer of Space Objects
Due to commercialisation of space activities, space objects may be subject to the transfer of title, transfer of ownership or transfer of operation and

18. Translated by Philippe Clere and Julien Mariez, Centre National d' Etudes Spatiales Legal Department, Paris, France; *Journal of Space Law*, Vol. 34, 2008, p. 453-470.
19. The Law on the Activities of Launching, Flight Operation or Guidance of Space Object, 2005 together with the Royal Implementing Decree 2008 constitute the Belgian Space Law.
20. Art. 11 of the Royal Decree 2005.
21. Art. 11(2) of the Royal Decree 2005.
22. The Austrian Federal Law on the Authorisation of Space Activities and the Establishment of a National Space Registry (Austrian Outer Space Act, adopted by the National Council on 6 December 2011, entered into force on 28 December 2011).

control. This transfer may be a national or international transfer. In the case of a national transfer there may not be much problem as the transferor and transferee are under the same jurisdiction of the State. Accordingly, the conditions of authorisation may be extended to the transferee simplifying the administrative process of transfer.[23] Problems may arise in case of an international transfer where the transferor and the transferee are under different jurisdictions. Since the original authorising State does not have jurisdiction over the transferee which is subject to the jurisdiction of a new State, the original State needs to be ensured that in case of a liability arising in future because of such a space object, it is to be absolved. The original authorising State also being the launching State, will further complicate the situation because international liability always vests with the launching State. In such a situation, the authorising State would need a guarantee of indemnification. This guarantee by the transferee will not be sufficient; rather, a guarantee from the State of the transferee would be required under whose jurisdiction the activity will be further carried.[24] Such a guarantee will ensure that the authorising State does not bear any financial liability in the future and that secondly, such activities are henceforth under the supervision of the appropriate State.

The Belgian Space Law has addressed both the situations of transfer. The transfer of authorised activities or real or personal rights which transfer the effective control of the space object is restricted under the Belgian Space Law. It may be transferred only with the Minister's prior authorisation. In the event of transfer, the condition levied at the time of granting authorisation to the initial licensee (transferor) becomes *mutatis mutandis* applicable to the prospective transferee.[25] The Minister may impose conditions to the transfer; authorisations which are binding on either the transferee operator, or the transferor operator, or both. This power has been vested mainly to modify the authorisation condition with the changed circumstances.

Interstate transfer is generally not permitted but in the case of a specific agreement with the transferee State, the Minister may do so subject to a

---

23. See Michael Gerhard, "Transfer of Operation and Control with Respect to Space Objects: Problems of Responsibility and Liability of States", *German Journal of Air and Space Law*, ZIW 51.Jg.4/2002, p. 571-581.

    Also see, Michael Chatzipanagiotis, "Registration of Space Objects and Transfer of Ownership in Orbit", *German Journal of Air and Space Law*, ZIW 56.Jg.2/2007 p.229-238.

24. Ibid.

25. Art. 13(3) of the Belgium Act.

further agreement that the transferee State shall indemnify the Belgian State against any recourse against it under its international liabilities or claims for damages.[26]

Though Belgium has levied conditions on international transfer as well, other national space legislations are silent on it. But state practices do suggest that such a transfer is not unconditional.[27] Should India expressly prescribe the conditions of transfer both nationally as well as internationally?

Environmental Safeguards

Almost all the national space legislations have a due consideration for environment and are of the opinion that the space activities should not damage environmental health. Belgium and Austria have taken an extended provision. The Belgian Space Act necessitates for a three-stage environment impact assessment of pre-launch, post launch and in case of the return of space objects. On the other hand, the Austrian Space Act has made provisions for debris mitigation wherein an operator has to make provisions for space debris mitigation in accordance with the state-of-the-art technology. Internationally recognised guidelines for the mitigation of space debris have to be given due importance which means that the Space Debris Mitigation Guidelines 2002 of the Inter-Agency Space Debris Coordination Committee (IADC) and the UNCOPUOS Space Debris Mitigation Guidelines of 2007 are inherent parts of this domestic space legislation.

Registration of Space Objects

Once again, an element of universality has been experienced by all the spacefaring nations with regard to the registration process. The spacefaring nations have practiced a registration of space objects in the manner prescribed by the Registration Convention. They have made compulsory registration of space objects launched by them both in their national registry and UN registry. Some States have maintained a secondary registry for maintaining a record of space objects which they have launched for commercial purposes and over which they do not wish to retain jurisdiction as they have been registered in the registry of some other nation. The authorised participants

---

26. Art. 13(5) of the Belgium Act.
27. See Michael Gerhard, "Transfer of Operation and Control with respect to Space Objects: Problems of Responsibility and Liability of States", *German Journal of Air and Space Law*, ZlW 51.Jg.4/2002 at p. 577.

are under an obligation to furnish the necessary details from time to time. Any change or new information has to be communicated promptly.

Sanctions

All the national space legislations seems to agree that the violation of their Acts shall invite sanction but there has been variation in the degrees of the sanction. Some have even made the violation of the Act as a criminal offence. There has been a variation in practice with the monetary fine payable. Whereas Belgium has prescribed a fine of minimum of 25 euro to a maximum of 25,000 euro, Austria has prescribed the fine of a minimum of 20,000 euro to a maximum of 100,000 euro. Should the National Space Act of India prescribe a civil or a criminal sanction? Should the Sanction be monetary or imprisonment or both? What should be the minimum and maximum duration of the imprisonment and of the monetary fine?

Conclusion

There is no doubt that there is a lot to learn from the state practices towards the national space legislation but it must be kept in mind that the National Space Act of India should be drafted according to the Indian needs and requirement. The challenge in laying the draft lies in deciding the appropriate administrative authority for effective authorisation and supervision and a suitable dispute resolution mechanism. As the commercial exploration of space is going to increase in a magnificent manner with an increased participation from the private sector, a more specialised legislation shall be needed in the future depending upon the nature of the space activity, as the United States has done.

India has been one of the active spacefaring nations. The world is eyeing us every moment. Rather than India adopting any model for its national space legislation, it should emerge as a model fulfilling its domestic needs in accordance with the Constitutional and international obligations.

7. Perspectives on Global Space Transport that may Begin Operations in Due Course

SALIGRAM BHATT

Introduction

In this article, I presume that space transport will commence operation between various long distance points that today take 14 hours which then maybe could be reduced to two hours. The time to introduce space transport may take ten to fifteen years. Space transport may fly like modern big-size aircraft like Air Bus 757, Boeing 747 or Boeing 777. ICAO is actively involved in deliberations between experts, governments, international aviation and space industries, Airbus industries and the UN Committee on Outer Space that has in the ICAO Headquarters, Montreal, positioned a Director for ICAO Space Programme. It may be recalled that ICAO became involved in space exploration activities much after the space law was formulated by the UN Committee on Peaceful Uses of Space. Only after 1999 and later because of the global environment issues, did the ICAO begin sending its representatives for space conferences held by the UN. The UNISPACE III Conference in Vienna in 1999 made a strong recommendation for space benefits for humankind. The emphasis was on communication, television, education, meteorology and remote sensing of resources. Space communication did impact aircraft communication and navigation. Space transport has not been discussed until recently. The space launch systems have improved and become reusable. Meanwhile, some attempts have been made with success to land back space objects like normal aircraft. Thus, we see today that a single space object can be a spacecraft and also be an aircraft on landing. Whatever be the technology, these space transport objects fly fast between long-distance geographical points like modern heavy air transport aircraft like the Boeing 747 that can carry almost 600 passengers. The new idea is to combine aviation and space technology. The two legal regimes have to cooperate for safe and economic space-transport services in the sub-orbital space region. A new vision is needed for the use of air and outer space for global space transport. The private economic sector is ready for the commercial uses of space transport. It has to be a safe, orderly and economical operation with due concern for sustainable development. ICAO is very much concerned with the global environment issues and carbon emissions.

Needs of Space Transport

Space transport, like air transport, needs three areas. First, a safe spacecraft for the transport of cargo and human passengers. I take for granted that this technology is available. Nevertheless, we may have dummy space flights—say a dozen or two as test flights between two points on earth to assure the global community that safety is not of concern. Second, we need a few space launch airports to launch the spacecraft and land them safely as aircraft. Long-runway airports placed far from towns are more suited; like the new airport in Hyderabad. It is also centrally placed to connect passengers by aircraft to other big towns like Delhi, Mumbai, Chennai and Guwahati. The third area that we need to provide is the regulatory environment of the space law and the air law that regulate the space transport flights. I will discuss these two regimes that have to help the space transport operate.

Space Law Regime

Most thinkers on the air law and air transport have remained ignorant of the space law regime. I personally took up space law studies for my PhD Programme in JNU. Space law experts were unaware of the air law regime. So, until recently—by when the space exploration had reached 58 years—and the ICAO had called space and aviation experts in Montreal, did we consider that a marriage between the two regimes was needed to start the space transport that could produce a new revolution for long distance points on earth. Space transport can be wonderful between Los Angeles to Sydney in two hours; Hyderabad to LA; London to Johannesburg; Kuala Lumpur to LA; India to countries in South America, and so on.

Essentials of the Space Law Regime

Let me inform students of space transport that space law has many applications like communications, education, remote sensing of earth resources, etc. Space transport is yet another area that space exploration has made possible now. The global space law regime consists of just five treaties and five UN Declarations. These are: the Space Treaty of 1967, called OST, that seems like an overall umbrella like the Chicago Convention of 1944 in air transport; Rescue of Astronauts 1968; the international Liability Convention 1972; Registration of Space Objects 1975 and the Moon Agreement of

1979. The UN Declarations applicable for space exploration are stated as follows: The 1963 Declaration of Legal Principles (later incorporated in the OST); Direct TV Broadcast Earth Satellites 1982; Legal Principles Relating to Remote Sensing of Earth from Outer Space 1986; Principles for Use of Nuclear Power Sources in Outer Space 1992 and the 1999 Declaration on International Cooperation in Exploration and Use of Outer Space for the benefit and interest of all states, especially for the needs of the developing countries.

The Essentials of the Outer Space Treaty (OST)

The Preamble to the OST refers to great prospects before humankind, common interests of all humankind, benefits of all peoples, international cooperation for the use of space for peaceful purposes, development of mutual understanding and the promotion of friendly relations between the states and peoples. In this respect, the OST has all the potential benefits for humankind. It does not bar space transport. However, point-to-point space transport will be made with a bilateral agreement between two countries, as in the case of air transport. Various OST articles are mentioned here that govern space exploration. Article 1 provides for the freedom of space for exploration and use. Article 2 bars a national appropriation of space, the Moon and other celestial bodies. Article 3 says that the exploration and use of space is based on international law and the Charter of the UN. Article 4 prohibits the placing of nuclear weapons in orbit. Military personnel can be used for space works. Article 5 regards astronauts as envoys of humankind, to be helped in conditions of distress. Article 6 calls upon the states to bear international responsibility for national activities in outer space. Article 7 makes the launching states liable for the damage caused to another state by space objects. Article 8 gives to the launching state jurisdiction and control over the objects launched into outer space. Article 9 provides for international cooperation and mutual assistance for exploration and use of outer space, and to avoid harmful contamination and adverse changes in the environment of the Earth by the introduction of extraterrestrial matter. States also are to hold international consultations whenever needed to avoid the harmful activities. Article 10 permits the states to observe the flight of space objects, subject to mutual agreements. Article 11 calls upon the states to inform the Secretary-General regarding the nature of space activities. Article 12 permits the states to visit stations and space vehicles on the Moon and other celestial bodies on a basis of reciprocity. Article 13 has this treaty applied in case of the exploration and use by a single state or jointly with other states or intergovernmental organisations.

Other Space Treaties and UN Declarations

The 1968 Agreement provides for the rescue and return of astronauts. The 1972 Convention is concerned with the international liability for damage. The 1975 one deals with the registration of space objects. The 1979 Agreement applies itself to activities on the Moon and other celestial bodies. Among the UN Declarations, we refer to the 1982 Declaration for direct television broadcasts. The 1986 Declaration refers to the remote sensing of Earth from outer space. The 1992 Declaration is for the use of nuclear power sources. The 1999 Declaration is for an overall international cooperation in exploration and use of outer space for the benefit and interest of all countries, especially the developing countries.

Interpretations of Space Law for the Global Air Transport

We have seen the major objectives and legal principles of space law that have similarity with the air law regime that governs air transport. The emphasis in space law is on the new great prospects for humankind: promoting the common interests of humankind, common benefits and international cooperation and understanding. There is freedom to explore and use outer space; keep space as a province of humankind; apply the international law and UN Charter to space activities; bear international responsibility for the states in their space activities' make the states liable for the damages caused to other states and like aircraft, have jurisdiction and control over space objects; promote international cooperation between states in space activities and hold consultations. The UN Space Treaties provide for rescue and help to astronauts; ensure international liability for damage; have a convention for registration of space objects like aircraft registrations; ensure that the TV broadcasts are done properly and with due care for the interests of other states; make laws for remote sensing of natural resources and promote international cooperation for the common benefits of humankind. It seems, therefore, that the space law has been excellently drawn for the beginning of space transport. Air transport had to develop these cooperative legal principles over a long period between the Paris Convention of 1919 to the Chicago Convention on civil aviation of 1944. Today, civil aviation is privatised, works on market economy and has the private industry working with the public sector to promote global economic benefits. I see a complete harmony between the two legal regimes: of aviation based on the Chicago Convention of 1944 and the space law regime based on the space treaties and declarations. In the ICAO's recent conference on space transport, the President of the Council asked, "How important regulatory flexibility will be for future space flights while using the space law?" The Director of the ICAO-Space programme then said, "Global space governance (under the space law as described and the air law under the Chicago Convention), encompassing space economy (as in the Chicago Convention where the safety and economic development of aviation are of paramount consideration, so as in the space law economic benefits and common interests of humankind are the most important objectives), space security, space accessibility and space diplomacy."

Air Law Regime

We know that the modern air law regime flows from the Chicago Convention of 1944. This convention has met the needs of global air transport. It has created the ICAO for the governance and management of global airspace. It has a number of Annexes made to promote the safe and orderly development of aviation. It has a Transit Agreement that permits the aircraft to overfly foreign country airspace without landing. This analogy can apply to the space transport that has a similar objective of carriage of passengers and cargo. The Montreal Convention on Liability of Airlines for carriage of passengers and cargo can hold good for space transport. A separate liability convention is already there for the space objects. The registration regimes are similar in air law and space law. Joint operation by states for space transport is envisaged clearly in both the air law and space law regimes. It seems that due to the high costs involved, joint operations by the states will be economical. Similarly, the security conventions in air law will apply to the space transport as well.

Who will Manage Space Transport?

This paragraph is important for us to work out. But without getting perplexed, we need to go back to the premise that we are treating space transport like air transport. In the latter case also, we have various regulating agencies that are involved. So also for space transport. In the international sphere, we have the ICAO and the space division of the UN working together in coordination. The space division looks after the space law, whereas the ICAO takes care of the air law regime. At the national level, we have the ISRO responsible for space objects, space laws (ISRO is drafting a new Space Act India) and the DGCA which regulates the aviation regime. We may have a common Board or Governing Body for the governance of space transport. It may have members for aviation, space, security, safety, airports/spaceports, international relations, ICAO, Space Division of the UN, Aviation Industry and Space Industry. I personally feel that the time is ripe to introduce global space transport, provided that the technology is perfect and the operation tried and proved to be economical and safe.

8.   Manifesto for PSLV Privatisation*

SUSMITA MOHANTY

Introduction to India's Launch Vehicles
The Indian Space Research Organization (ISRO) has two Expendable Launch Vehicles (ELVs) in its fleet. One is the Polar Satellite Launch Vehicle (PSLV)[1] and the other is the Geosynchronous Satellite Launch Vehicle (GSLV).[2]

The PSLV is used to launch the Earth Observation (EO) satellites in the Sun Synchronous Orbits (SSO), both for India and for foreign clients. It has multiple variants and has also been used for launching India's robotic orbiter missions to the Moon and Mars. Here is an overview of the PSLV flight record since its debut launch in September 1993:

Total launches: 30
PSLV: 11
PSLV-CA: 10
PSLV-XL: 9

Successes: 29
PSLV: 9
PSLV-CA: 10
PSLV-XL: 9

Failures: 1
Partial failures: 1

where,
PSLV = standard version with boosters

---

*   The author would like to thank Mr Shabarinath Nair, currently an intern at the Earth2Orbit, for researching and providing the input for section Privatisation of the Japanese H2 Launch System: Highlights.

1.   https://en.wikipedia.org/wiki/Polar_Satellite_Launch_Vehicle, as viewed on 17 August 2015.
2.   https://en.wikipedia.org/wiki/Geosynchronous_Satellite_Launch_Vehicle, as viewed on 17 August 2015.

PSLV-CA = Core Alone version without strap-on boosters

PSLV-XL = High Performance version

The GSLV was primarily developed to launch the INSAT[3] class of satellites into the Geosynchronous Transfer Orbits (GTO). This ELV is still under development. The GSLV has attempted eight launches till date, since its first launch in 2001 through its most recent launch in 2014. The ninth launch is scheduled for end-August 2015. It has two variants, the Mk.I and Mk.II. the GSLV flight record as of 5 August 2015 is as follows:

Total launches	**8** (6 Mk.I, 2 Mk.II)
Successes	**3** (2 Mk.I, 1 Mk.II)
Failures	**4** (3 Mk.I, 1 Mk.II)
Partial failures	**1** (Mk.I)

As of 2014, the PSLV has launched 71 spacecraft (31 Indian and 40 foreign satellites) into a variety of orbits. It is a highly mature and reliable rocket in its class. The main international competitor for the PSLV has been the Russian Dnepr.[4] The Dnepr is an intercontinental ballistic missile (ICBM) converted into a commercial launch vehicle that uses boosters from the declassified Russian stockpile making it the cheapest launch option in the international market. Other competitors of the PSLV include the American Minotaur-I[5] (also an ICBM convert), and the relatively new launchers: Vega[6] from Europe (first flight February 2012) and Epsilon from Japan[7] (first flight September 2013).

There are rumours that the Russian launcher Dnepr might not be available as readily anymore. There are reports suggesting that Russia is developing a lighter-lift variant of the Soyuz that will target the growing small satellite launch market. Additionally, the new Vega rocket from Europe will likely give the PSLV stiff competition in the years ahead given that it is built, launched, and marketed by Arianespace—the dominant player in the commercial launch space.

---

3   https://en.wikipedia.org/wiki/Indian_National_Satellite_System, as viewed on 17 August 2015.

4.   http://www.kosmotras.ru/en/zapuski/, as viewed on 17 August 2015.

5.   https://en.wikipedia.org/wiki/Minotaur_(rocket_family), as viewed on 17 August 2015.

6.   http://www.esa.int/Our_Activities/Launchers/Launch_vehicles/Vega, as viewed on 17 August 2015.

7.   http://global.jaxa.jp/projects/rockets/epsilon/, as viewed on 17 August 2015.

As per reports released by the Indian government in July 2015,[8] India has earned about US$ 100 million launching 45 foreign satellites till date and that the revenue from its commercial space missions is poised to grow with another 28 foreign satellites planned to be put into orbit between 2015 and 2017. The first foreign payload was launched by the PSLV in May 1999. Thus, it has made a total revenue of US$ 100 million in nearly a decade and a half. There was no mention by the government of how much profit has accrued through the cumulative launch of those commercial payloads since 1999. It has probably been very modest, at best. Compare the PSLV commercial revenue between 1999–2015 to the annual global market for the commercial payloads at US$ 3 billion and you find that while the PSLV record is laudable on the national level, on a global scale, it is still miniscule.[9]

The International Launch Landscape

There were more successful space launches in 2014 than in any year since 1992, with Russia, the United States and China being responsible for more than 80 per cent of the global launch activity. Russia had the most liftoffs with 36 orbital launch attempts of which 34 were deemed complete successes. The United States came in second with 23 space launches, with all but one reaching its intended target. The Chinese rockets scored 16-for-16 satellite launches in 2014.

The European-built Ariane-5 and Vega launchers achieved a 100 per cent success rate in 2014 with 7 missions. Japan and India each conducted 4 successful space launches with the H-2A and PSLV/GSLV respectively. Israel put a satellite into orbit with a Shavit rocket in its only launch of the year.

There were 92 space launches worldwide in 2014, and 90 of the missions at least reached orbit. By comparison, there had been 81 space launch attempts in 2013.[10]

The global space transportation business primarily serves the national governments and large commercial customers. Launching the government payloads constitutes the largest market segment at nearly $100 billion a year and is dominated by the United Launch Alliance (a joint venture of the Lockheed

---

8   http://www.thehindu.com/sci-tech/science/india-earns-100-million-launching-45-foreign-satellites/article7452376.ece, as viewed on 17 August 2015.

9   http://www.huffingtonpost.in/2015/07/23/isro_0_n_7855336.html, as viewed on 17 August 2015.

10. http://spaceflightnow.com/2015/01/04/2014s-launch-tally-highest-in-two-decades/, as viewed on 17 August 2015.

Martin Space Systems and Boeing Defense, Space & Security) in the United States and by Arianespace worldwide. The commercial payloads market is valued at approximately $3 billion a year and is dominated by Arianespace, with over 50% of the market share, followed by Russian launchers.[11]

The commercial launch service providers in 2014 booked 19 orders open to competitive bidding for the satellites to be launched into geostationary orbit. Of the 19 commercial launch contracts competitively awarded in 2014, Arianespace and SpaceX took home nine apiece.[12]

The Growing Small Satellite Launch Market

A presentation at the recent Small Satellite (Smallsat) Conference[13] in Utah in August 2015 by Carlos Niederstrasser and Warren Frick of the Orbital ATK identified more than 20 smallsat launch vehicles, from the existing Pegasus and Minotaur-1 of USA to concepts still in the early design phase. However, most of the presentations in the launch session of the conference were about secondary payload, or rideshare opportunities. Hitching a ride to orbit on a larger launch vehicle remains the primary way most smallsats are launched today. Some launches have taken the launching of smallsats to extremes. A Minotaur launch in November 2013 carried 31 smallsats from 20 different operators.[14]

The Indian PSLV has in the past few years started to frequently launch several smallsats as secondary payloads on each launch. This trend began with the launch of a cluster of 10 satellites in April 2008, two of which were Indian payloads and the remaining 8 were foreign smallsats ranging from 0.75–8.0 kg.[15]

It is this growing market of the secondary smallsat launches that presents a significant opportunity for the Indian PSLV rocket. For a few decades now, Russian launchers have dominated the market. The new Vega rocket from Europe is starting to gain prominence as well. SpaceX has its fair share of these launches despite being a heavy-lifter.

---

11. https://en.wikipedia.org/wiki/Private_spaceflight and http://www.wsj.com/articles/SB118273597464946694, as viewed on 17 August 2015.
12. http://spacenews.com/chart-arianespace-spacex-battled-to-a-draw-for-2014-launch-contracts/, as viewed on 17 August 2015.
13. www.smallsat.org/
14. http://spacenews.com/launching-smallsats-and-herding-cats/, as viewed on 17 August 2015.
15. https://en.wikipedia.org/wiki/Polar_Satellite_Launch_Vehicle, as viewed on 17 August 2015.

One of the new smallsat launch companies, Rocket Labs, has started to take advance bookings on the future launches of its Electron rocket for the launches starting in the third quarter of 2016 and extending into 2019.[16] Customers can buy slots on the company's website for 1U and 3U cubesats. Prices range from $70,000 to $80,000 for a 1U cubesat and $200,000 to $250,000 for a 3U cubesat.

The PSLV can successfully compete with the established and emerging launch providers if the Indian government liberalises the space economy. For this, the ISRO will have to accelerate its plans for the PSLV privatisation announced by the last ISRO Chairman Mr. K. Radhakrishnan in 2012[17] and reiterated by the new ISRO Chairman Mr. A. S. Kiran Kumar after he took over in 2015.

India can learn from the American, European and Japanese launch vehicle privatisation models and could choose a hybrid model drawing from their experience and outcome. The ISRO can then adopt a Public Private Partnership (PPP) model that is applicable in the context of the Indian space industry.

It is beyond the scope of this paper to discuss the launch sector privatisation of all of these geographies. The following two sections will present an overview of the privatisation of the European and Japanese launch systems.

Privatisation of the European Ariane Launch System: Highlights
Arianespace SA is a European multinational company founded in 1980 as the world's first commercial launch service provider.[18] The European Space Agency (ESA), an intergovernmental organisation with 22 European member states, created Arianespace, a company that was to be operated commercially after the initial hardware and launch facilities had been developed with government funding.

Arianespace flies the heavy-lift Ariane-5 rocket, a Europeanised version of Russia's Soyuz booster and the Italian-led Vega launcher from the French-run Guiana Space Center on the northern coast of South America. Arianespace went on to become the most successful commercial launch

---

16. http://spacenews.com/rocket-lab-booking-smallsat-launches-online/, as viewed on 17 August 2015.
17. http://www.ndtv.com/india-news/indias-rocket-launch-business-is-open-to-industry-490602, as viewed on 17 August 2015.
18. https://en.wikipedia.org/wiki/Arianespace, as viewed on 17 August 2015.

provider in the world. By 1995, Arianespace had launched its 100th satellite and by 1997 it had launched its 100th Ariane rocket.

For 35 years, the Arianespace ownership was divided among the French Space Agency CNES, the prime contractor Airbus and several subcontractors spread across Europe. Earlier this year, in June 2015, the French government announced its intention to sell its nearly 35% stake in Arianespace to a Joint Venture (JV) called Airbus Safran Launchers (ASL) formed by the Airbus Defense & Space and the Ariane rocket engine manufacturer, Safran.[19] This will give the ASL control of 74 per cent shares of the France-based launch provider. More than a quarter of the Arianespace shares will remain in the hands of smaller subcontractors spread across France, Germany, Belgium, Italy, Spain, Switzerland, Sweden, the Netherlands, Norway and Denmark.

For the first time in Europe's space programme, the new Ariane-6 rocket will be designed by the private sector as opposed to the CNES, and will be funded by a PPP between the ASL and ESA. The CNES will continue to be responsible for the ground systems at the French Guiana launch base.

The move is a significant milestone in the shakeup of the European launch sector and comes as a cost-cutting measure with a goal of creating a more efficient supply chain for Europe's Ariane launchers in response to the competition from newcomers to the market like SpaceX. SpaceX[20] is a new space transportation company founded in 2002 in California. It has directly benefitted from NASA's Commercial Orbital Transportation Services (COTS)[21] programme. NASA's COTS programme was created as a response to the Space Shuttle fleet retirement in 2011. NASA needed a replacement ferry for the humans and the cargo to the International Space Station (ISS) in a compressed time frame. The COTS programme is exemplary in how to build newer, better, cheaper launch systems by engaging the private industry.

The COTS programme allows the private entrepreneurs to lead and direct their efforts with NASA, providing technical and financial assistance. The COTS enables the industry and NASA to co-invest and co-develop new space transportation systems. SpaceX's Falcon 9 v1.0 development costs are estimated at US$ 300 million. NASA has admitted that if it had developed

---

19. http://spaceflightnow.com/2015/06/11/france-to-privatize-its-arianespace-shares/, as viewed on 17 August 2015.

20. http://www.spacex.com/, as viewed on 17 August 2015.

21. http://www.nasa.gov/offices/c3po/about/c3po.html, as viewed on 17 August 2015.

this rocket using a traditional cost-plus-contract approach, the development costs would have been more than US$3 billion.[22]

Privatisation of the Japanese H2 Launch System: Highlights
The first in the H2 series of rockets was developed by the National Space Development Agency (NASDA) in order to make Japan self-reliant in launching the larger satellites into orbit. The H2 rocket was used seven times between 1994 and 1999 with five successful flights. In order to overcome the reliability and cost issues, the H2A was developed to succeed the H2.[23]

H2A is one of the two launch systems operated by the Mitsubishi Heavy Industries (MHI) for the Japanese Space Exploration Agency (JAXA). MHI has launched the H2A rockets for missions to put satellites into the Geosynchronous orbit, a lunar orbiter and an interplanetary probe to Venus. H2A was first launched in 2001 and as of now has flown 28 times with 27 successful missions.[24]

The privatisation of the H2A began with the shifting of the production and launch operation of the H2A in 2007. The lunar orbiter SELENE mission was the first mission after privatisation and the 13th flight of the H2A rocket. The organisational responsibilities of the JAXA and the MHI for the launch of the H2A launch system are as follows.[25]

JAXA	MHI
Safety review	Programme Management
Flight Safety	Mission Integration
Ground Safety	Vehicle Manufacturing
Range Safety	Mission Modification & Technical Support
Launch Facility Maintenance	Launch Operations

The first rocket developed by the JAXA and MHI partnership is the H2B rocket for launching the H2 Transfer Vehicle (HTV). The HTV is a cargo ferry used to transfer supplies and logistics to the orbiting ISS. The H2B was first flown in 2009 and as of now has been launched successfully four times. The HTV to the ISS has been the primary payload on each occasion.

22. https://www.quora.com/Is-SpaceX-now-the-best-rocket-making-company-in-history and http://www.nasa.gov/sites/default/files/files/Section403%28b%29CommercialMark etAssessmentReportFinal.pdf, as viewed on 17 August 2015.
23. https://en.wikipedia.org/wiki/H-II, as viewed on 17 August 2015.
24. https://en.wikipedia.org/wiki/H-IIA, as viewed on 17 August 2015.
25. http://h2a.mhi.co.jp/service/manual/pdf/manual.pdf, as viewed on 17 August 2015.

The H2B can launch a payload of 8 tonnes to the GTO compared with the payload of 4 to 6 tonnes by its predecessor, the H2A.

For the H2B development, previously proven technologies were adopted to minimise the cost and risk. The JAXA carried out the preliminary design, ground facility and new technologies development, while the MHI was primarily responsible for manufacturing. After the third successful launch of the H2B, an agreement was made between the JAXA and the MHI by which the MHI would take the entire role in the H2B launches.

The MHI is currently planning to develop the next version of the H2A/B model. The primary objectives include the availability and affordability for a better and easier access to the space transportation systems. The MHI intends to drastically reduce costs by applying its expertise in the domestic cutting-edge industries to its aerospace vehicles.[26]

The concluding section below draws inspiration from the European, Japanese and American experiences and proposes a manifesto for the privatisation of India's PSLV.

Manifesto for PSLV Privatisation

- Think Space 2.0! Think in 50 to 100 year cycles, not in 5 to 10 year cycles.
- Develop a commercial mindset, an international outlook.
- Leverage the new government's "Make in India" and "Ease of Doing Business" campaigns. Minimise red tape; standardise procedures, streamline approval cycles and establish objective performance criteria. Publish clear launch manifests, user manuals and unambiguous pricing. Promote Indian space start-ups developing and providing products and services for the launch sector.
- Phase-A: Create a JV comprising a prime contractor, engine maker and other vendors that supply components and subsystems to the ISRO's ELV programme. Hand over production, assembly, launch and marketing of the PSLV to this JV. ISRO can continue to operate the ground systems at the Satish Dhawan Space Centre (SHAR), ISRO's spaceport, and run all the necessary safety checks.
- Phase-B: Bet on young entrepreneurs and new companies. Introduce a NASA COTS-like programme to foster the private entrepreneurs to develop and demonstrate cargo space transportation capabilities. The

---

26. https://www.mhi.co.jp/technology/review/pdf/e501/e501063.pdf, as viewed on 17 August 2015.

private companies and ISRO should co-invest and co-develop new space transportation systems that will not only be used for satellite launches, but also for ferrying cargo and humans to space.

- Enact a Commercial Space Launch Act to encourage commercial space transportation systems and enable the Indian industry to build and operate ELVs and RLVs including future space planes for the space tourism industry.

- Establish a Commercial Spaceport. Use the SHAR for government launches. Develop a separate dedicated spaceport for commercial launches.

- Create a safety and regulatory framework to enable a private access to space. The Indian Civil Aviation Ministry should follow in the footsteps of the American Federal Aviation Administration (FAA) and establish a pragmatic safety and regulatory framework in collaboration with the industry to enable private space planes, both for humans and cargo. It will begin with a 'learning period' during which the new laws and regulations will be put to test and then fine-tuned over time.

- Replace the Space Commission with a new entity with a particular emphasis on deregulation and privatisation encouraging, to the maximum extent possible, the fullest commercial use of space. This new entity should be led by industry stalwarts, while the Department of Space (DOS) can continue to be headed by the ISRO chief.

9. Space Law for Space Commerce or Vice Versa: A Chicken-and-Egg Situation for Space Commerce in India?

NARAYAN PRASAD

Activities in outer space have tremendously evolved since the launch of the first satellite in 1957 as a front for national prestige and pride to a truly commercial arena of providing services based on satellites. Projections in the last few years have indicated that the global satellite industry revenues have grown from $144.4 billion in 2008 to $195.2 billion in 2013.[1] With the average growth rates of more than 5% year on year over the last decade, the global space industry has enabled tremendous advances in the way people use space in their daily lives.

While there was a period of failed business models in the 1990s in the sector, there has been renewed interest from Venture Capitalists (VC) to invest in space with several companies such as OneWeb, SpaceX, SkyBox Imaging, Planet Labs, Spire, etc. raising millions of dollars in building swarms of satellites offering commercial services. With such trends in the global space sector, one of the key questions lying before the Government of India should be as to how to enable the Indian industry in tapping a larger share in the international marketplace.

While the Indian Space Research Organisation (ISRO) works on a shoestring budget, the Government of India needs to recognise the fact that the heritage it has created over the course of five decades has tremendous commercial potential. In order to tap the commercial potential of manufacturing satellites and launch vehicles, the Government needs to recognise the fundamental need for the creation of an ecosystem and an environment of certainty to encourage the investors and to enable the risk-taking scenarios as it has done in several other sectors since the 1990s.

Understanding the Indian Space Value Chain
The space sector can be divided into upstream and downstream with the former entailing manufacturing of satellites, parts, subsystems, launch

---

1. The Tauri Group, "State of the Satellite Industry Report", *Satellite Industry Association*, September 2014, http://www.sia.org/wp-content/uploads/2014/05/SIA_2014_SSIR.pdf.

vehicles and the latter provisioning services based on satellites such as satellite TV, imagery, communications, etc. *Table 1* provides an overview of the space industry subsectors.[2] The value chain is currently dominated by government entities and participation of the commercial space industry is solely limited to the supply of parts, components and subsystems manufacturing.

In the present model of engaging the local space industry in India, there is no extensive commercial exploitation of the space infrastructure due to a lack of deregulation and privatisation of the country's space sector. In comparison, any advanced spacefaring nation has most of these blocks in the value chain privatised, which enables the multiplier effect by creating a strong economic impact.

As an economic assessment example of enabling the private space industry, the US space industry satellite manufacturers captured nearly 52% of the global satellite revenues in 2010. The US satellite manufacturing industry employed 26,611 private-sector workers in 2010, while the US commercial launch industry employed 49,195 private-sector workers.[3]

While there are 500 Small and Medium Scale Enterprises (SMEs) working with ISRO,[4] none of them have gone on to achieve turnkey capabilities in the space sector. This inability of the Indian space industry in providing turnkey solutions independent of the Government lowers the space competitiveness index of the country critically in the eyes of the international space commerce arena.

The current major challenge for the Government is to identify and pursue active strategies in the short, medium and long-term for not only increasing the space competitiveness of the local space industry, but in creating a roadmap for the ISRO to phase out the development of routine satellites for communications, imagery and navigational needs and focus instead on developing state-of-the-art futuristic technologies and missions.

---

2. Kelly Whealan-George, "The Projected U.S. Economic Impacts of the Space Industry 2030", *Embry-Riddle Aeronautical University*, October 2013, http://commons.erau.edu/cgi/viewcontent.cgi?article=1000&context=ww-economics-social-sciences.

3. Glennon Harrison, "The Commercial Space Industry and Launch Market", *Congressional Research Service*, April 20, 2012, http://www.law.umaryland.edu/marshall/crsreports/crsdocuments/R42492_04202012.pdf.

4. "ISRO to Focus on R&D, Industries' Space Pie to Be Scaled Up", *The Hindu*, accessed June 30, 2015, http://www.thehindu.com/sci-tech/science/isro-to-focus-on-rd-industries-space-pie-to-be-scaled-up/article4991988.ece.

Table 1: Space Industry Subsectors and Stakeholders

Satellite Services	Manufacturing	Launch	Ground Equipment
Consumer Services • Satellite TV • Satellite Ration • Satellite Broadband	Satellite Manufacturing	Launch Services	**Network Equipment** • Gateways • Control Stations • Very Small Aperture Terminals (VSAT)
Fixed Satellite Services • Transponder Agreements • Managed Network Services	Parts, Components & Subsystem Manufacturing	Launch Vehicles Services	**Consumer Equipment** • Direct Broadcast Satellite (DBS) Dishes • Mobile Satellite Terminals (including Satellite Phones) • Digital Audio Radio Service (DARS) Equipment • Navigation Stand-Alone Hardware
Mobile Satellite Services • Mobile Data • Mobile Voice			
Remote Sensing			
Space Flight Management Services			
Private/Commercial Industry	Government/ ISRO/DoS	Quasi-Government	

Enabling Space Commerce in India

The space agencies in Europe and USA have matured to have mandated the development of traditional satellites and launch vehicles via the private industry and the governmental institutions have matured to work towards benchmarking and providing oversight rather than increasing their scope of work from scoping a particular programme to a service implementation of the same at the end. This approach has led to the creation of a strong industry ecosystem in these countries enabling them to not only cater to the local demand but also to provide them with an opportunity to participate in the global marketplace.

The Government of India must look to create umbrella programmes in technology as well as overhaul the very way governance is done in the space sector for an overhauling of the current stance to take a full advantage of the technological heritage and the investments it has sustained in building up the capacity in the past few decades.

While the umbrella programmes enabling the industries can be Public–Private Partnerships (PPPs), creation of business incubation centres/space parks for SME development, turnkey technology transfer programmes, creation of national funds for industry-led research in space, etc., the governance aspect needs to address the creation of transparency in decision-making, avoidance of conflicts of interest, time-bound decision-making, focusing on the ease of enabling business, clarity in regulatory environment, etc.

The only way to capture a larger portion of the global revenues in the space sector for India is to enable the industry to integrate itself with the globalised world. A typical example of such an integration which the ISRO can emulate for capturing greater revenue shares in the launch market is that of the emergence of Ariane Space as a PPP. The ISRO can look to create a consortium of vendors that have been working to produce its workhorse, the Polar Satellite Launch Vehicle (PSLV), to enable the industry to gain larger volumes in production leading to a bigger business on one side, while the image and reputation that the PSLV has created in the international marketplace can be leveraged to provide more frequent launch opportunities for foreign satellites.

One of the ways to focus on the enabling of space commerce can well be to set up an Office of Space Commercialisation by the ISRO that shall focus on the emergence of India as a leader in world space commerce. The US Department of Commerce has established such an entity that fosters conditions for the economic growth and technological advancement of the US commercial space industry and has been successful in reducing legal, policy and institutional impediments to space commerce, promoting growth in the export of space-related goods and services.[5]

However, if more such avenues in space commerce need to be explored at the turnkey level, critical issues such as technology transfer, Intellectual

---

5.   "U.S. Leadership In Space Commerce", *U.S. Department of Commerce: Office of Space Commercialization*, March 2007, http://www.space.commerce.gov/wp-content/uploads/NOAA-2007-Space-Commercialization-Strategic-Plan-6-pages.pdf.

Property Rights (IPR), export control, liabilities, insurance and several other issues need to addressed. These factors shall influence the mood in the marketplace and thereby the investors' confidence. They not only affect the local ecosystem but also have a distinct effect on the perception of the investors/customers in the global marketplace. Therefore, enabling the space commerce is fundamentally intertwined with having a strong foundation in space law.

Space Law: The Indian Perspective

In its current stance, the space value chain in India has a governmental dominance or quasi-governmental requirements over all space activities both upstream and downstream. Although India has pursued space activities for over five decades, there has been no political mandate in pursuing a national space legislation to this day.

Currently, the Department of Space (DoS) has chosen to allow private participation in satellite-based services (either SatCom or remote sensing) via policies (SatCom policy/Remote Sensing Data Policy). These policies provide a cover on the procedures and processes that need to be followed for participation. However, they provide no insights on key issues such as timelines, liabilities, oversight procedures, etc., which have a fundamental impact on driving participation of non-governmental entities.

One of the key reasons for this lack of drive within the legal and political fronts could well be the monopolistic nature of this sector in India. The ISRO is the only organisation in the country getting government investments to develop space capabilities and the industry structure has traditionally remained in being vendors within the system rather than in being turnkey solution providers to suit the national requirements. With such an organisational structure, the activities pursued in outer space lie within the mandate of the government with the industry ecosystem feeding off the taxpayer money pumped into the sector that could have been used for creating upstream capacities.

Therefore, the requirement on the part of the government regulatory and oversight bodies for monitoring the actions of the private/non-governmental bodies related to the activities in the outer space are non-existent. Though India is a signatory to the international treaties on outer space, this may well be one of the fundamental reasons behind the legislators not taking a proactive approach to the development of a comprehensive space law for the pursuit of space activities in the country.

In a recent development, the ISRO has announced that it has been working on drafting a national space legislation.[6] However, there has been no public tabling of any details on the contents of the draft as yet. It remains critical that the National Space Legislation of India acts as an enabler for space commerce rather than just to cover the international treaty obligations of the country.

Space Law Enabling Space Commerce

It is important that in addition to fulfilling the international treaty obligations, the procedural aspects of enabling the space commerce should find their foundation in a national space legislation and encourage the private space industry to engage in a larger way both nationally and internationally. The templates of such enabling legislations and procedural aspects are already available such as the Commercial Space Transportation Act from the United States which can be studied to import some of its critical aspects into the Indian scenario.

A comprehensive space legislation for India should provide a reassessment of the current policies (SatCom, remote sensing data) and also provide a cover on the issues that have currently not been addressed such as authorisation, satellite operations frequency allocation (for remote sensing), licensing of satellite systems for the LEO small satellites and other non-SatCom policy proposals made by the private industry.

Given the current stance of the Indian space ecosystem, it appears that the Government of India needs to work on both the enabling of the local industry in reaching a turnkey solution capability status as well as on providing a legal blanket for these industries to assess and align their processes, interests and business models to encourage the space commerce.

The establishment of a comprehensive space legislation alongside the well-defined and transparent procedural aspects of commerce will promote a stable and predictable policy and regulatory environment that contributes to the success of the commercial space efforts, the entry of new entrepreneurs (including those not traditionally associated with the space

---

6. Madhumathi D. S, "ISRO Chairman: New Space Roadmap Soon, but Tackling the Backlog Comes First", *The Hindu*, July 1, 2015, http://www.thehindu.com/sci-tech/science/isro-chairman-new-space-roadmap-soon-but-tackling-the-backlog-comes-first/article7375129.ece.

activities), support a policy and procurement environment that supports the private sector intellectual property and the creation of new markets for the space goods and services.

Conclusion

The linking up of a well-established legal foundation with space commerce remains critically important to the building of an industry ecosystem that provides a value in time and money for the international customers to choose India as their destination for space commerce.

If the Government of India chooses to take such steps in building up an extensive ecosystem in supporting the legal and entrepreneurial environments, it might very well enable the Indian industry to take up a turnkey development of spacecraft and rockets, leading to a foreseeable increase in the competitiveness of the Indian industry in the global marketplace.

This path in retrospect to the current scenario can create a multiplier effect with some substantial benefits including

- Creation of new jobs in the highly skilled labour market being created in the private space industry in India.
- Avoidance of the taxpayer money circulation within the ecosystem and instead, having foreign customers procuring the turnkey products and services from the Indian industry.
- Reversal of brain drain from the country.
- Adding an edge to India's foreign policy drives with space as a major emerging tool in relationship fostering and development.
- Enabling the space technology to be used as tool in the defence of the country and in enabling the armed forces to engage with the private space industry in creating a strong local ecosystem for the indigenous procurement of defence products and services.
- Creating more Foreign Direct Investments (FDI) via the 'Make in India' and the 'Digital India' campaigns.

10. Policy Framework for Commercial Space Activities[1]

ASHOK G. V.

The trends across the world have led us to understand that the private sector participation in space activities is as inevitable, as it is conducive to optimise the innovation and ensure a meaningful application of space assets to address the human needs.[2] India has demonstrated its vision as well as prowess in the space sector, through its recent achievements with the Moon and Mars missions. The private sector participation in these achievements has been largely been as tier 2 and tier 3 vendors to the Indian Space Research Organization (ISRO). However, an increasing consensus among the various stakeholders reminds that if we can enhance the private sector participation in space, then we can slingshot the efficacy of our space operations by many leaps forward.

Perhaps an unexciting, yet important factor in this potential collaboration between the private space sector and the Indian State, is the kind of policy that will define the foundation of the relationship. The narrative around this topic, begins with the important reminder that under the provisions of the Outer Space Treaty, India is responsible for all the space activities that arise within its territory or mandate.[3] With this being the major responsibility for the State, it is incumbent that any policy towards the private sector participation envisages a robust yet vision-oriented regulatory body. No doubt, the SATCOM Policy envisages a regulatory function for the Department of Space.[4]

However, given that the ISRO is answerable to the Department of Space and given that the ISRO itself remains a key player in space activities, the private sector has legitimate concerns about the existing regulator also being a competitor. It is perhaps for this reason that the regulatory body under

---

1. The author acknowledges the valuable contribution of Mr. Narayan Prasad, Director, Dhruva Space and Ms. Sai Apabharana K.M. and M. Priya Subramaniam, Students of the Bangalore Institute of Legal Studies for their valuable inputs and research.
2. Highlights in Space 2006. Pg.105
3. Article VII of Outer Space Treaty - Treaty on Principles Governing the Activities of States in the Exploration and Use of Outer Space, Including the Moon and Other Celestial Bodies
4. See provisions of Article 3.7.4 of the SATCOM Policy

the Commercial Space Launch Act, 1984 in the USA is the Secretary of Transport and not the NASA.[5]

If the policy going forward continues to extend a regulatory role to the Department of Space, then it inspires a skeptical view of the Indian market for the space activities, on the ground that the regulatory atmosphere is hostile to healthy competition. It is important that the Indian State reflects on this while defining a regulator, as to who the regulator will be and what kind of powers, duties (deadlines for grant of authorisations, framework for exercise of discretion, etc.) and functions it will have and whether it will also go to the root of how much confidence the investors will have in investing in the Indian Space Industry.

The other aspect that India has to touch upon is the ownership of space assets. This area of space policy is invariably connected with the questions of national security, for the reason that the State would like to have a mechanism that allows a ready control of the space assets in times of national security crises like war and terror attacks, which is obviously a problem when there is private ownership (jurisprudence requires nationalisation or expropriation to be founded upon non-arbitrary and reasonable procedures with the payment of fair compensation). The issue of the ownership of space assets is also connected with the liability for debris and damage caused by the space assets as well as defining a rational tax regime around the sale of space assets. For example, under the provisions of Section 5 of the Central Sales Tax Act, 1956, the high-sea sales are exempt from the purview of sales tax. Given that space is outside the purview of the Indian Territory, the sale of space assets would likely fall within the exemption envisaged under Section 5 of the CST Act. In such a scenario, disallowing the ownership of space assets and allowing only the transfer of licenses to operate the space assets would confer the authority to tax, but would also deter the investors. Thus a comprehensive policy around the ownership of space assets that addresses these competing interests would have to be a part of the overall policy.

Liability and Insurance is another critical aspect for the policy to consider. While the sovereign immunity principles give a considerable immunity to the ISRO from a tortuous liability domestically, the international law is far more stringent in its approach, especially where the space objects

---

5.   Bonnie E. Fought, "Legal Aspects of the Commercialization of Space Transportation Systems", *Berkeley Technology Law Journal*, Article 4, Volume 3, Issue 1, Spring, January 1988, http://scholarship.law.berkeley.edu/cgi/viewcontent.cgi?article=1068&context=btlj, Visited 15 May 2015.

inflict damage upon the living and non-living objects on earth.[6] As part of the process to address this issue and to meaningfully ensure diligence, the space policy will have to define a public insurance scheme on the lines of the Public Liability Insurance Act and also stipulate negligence in space activities as offences with the proportionate punitive measures.

From the commercial operators' perspective, another key topic is inter-party waivers or cross-waivers in the relationships between the payload owners, launch-service providers, customers, sub-contractors, etc. There is a precedent for suggesting that the liability waivers should be mandatory in this ecosystem of parties in the transactions surrounding the space activities.[7] While such waivers could achieve immunity from contractual damages, they will not take away the right to seek damages under the principles of tort. Not recognising the waiver of the right to seek damages for torts will lead the ISRO to enjoy a competitive advantage as it enjoys the sovereign immunity. Thus, any policy on space activities has to take a stand on whether the tortuous liability can also be waived through the contractual waiver clauses and disclaimers.

The next leg of the discussion ventures into the questions of National Security, particularly in the case of satellite imaging. This is also closely linked to the question of a regulator for space activities. While satellite imaging is now a global reality, one way of ensuring the national security interests for satellite imaging activities by the Indian space sector players, is to insist for a periodic filing of returns of the coordinates photographed and to insist that no transaction in imaging will be allowed, except with the consent of the regulator. With legislations like the Official Secrets Act already in force, the issue is not so much about poor policy leading to compromised national security interests as much as it is about creating the right enforcement mechanisms. To this end, The SCOMET list will have to be suitably amended to specify the kind of technology and data that can be transacted in and the end-user certificates must be insisted upon wherever the data or technology with a bearing on national security is sought to be transacted in.

Last but not the least, the technology transfer policies need a substantial revamp. While the precedents abroad are explicit about the policy framework

6. Article II of the Convention on International Liability for Damage Caused by Space Objects stipulates an absolute liability for any damage on the surface of the earth or to aircrafts. Article III prescribes a fault-based liability for the damage caused by space objects to other space objects.
7. Chapter 509: Commercial Space Launch Activities

for the sale and license of governmental technology,[8] the present technology transfer policies are grossly lacking in terms of such clarity. On the other hand, the existing technology transfer policy concludes by stating that no uniform policy can be prescribed and a situation-specific methodology has to be evolved to govern the individual transactions in a technology transfer.

Even the data from the ISRO's space assets is difficult to access. It would thus be useful for the policymakers to consider formulating a comprehensive National G.I. Policy.[9] The Indian state has already made some progress in this direction[10] and we believe that this trend of becoming conscious of the opportunities around the data generated by the space assets is encouraging and should pick up momentum.

Any attempts at misuse or misappropriation of the technology so transferred can be curbed by the introduction of punitive provisions in the impending space legislation as well as by developing strong contract clauses in respect of the technology transfer that stipulate stringent prohibitions around the sub-licensing or sub-transfer of the technology in any manner whatsoever. But, the mere chance of misuse should not come in the way of innovation, which we all know is better facilitated with a liberal sharing of ideas and technology.

The analysis and discussions in this paper only provide a preview of the broad range of topics that any policy for commercial space activities has to address. We anticipate that to meaningfully encourage and enhance the private sector participation in India's space programmes, what is required is not just a single legislation but a broad range of legislative exercises including amendments to the many existing legislations ranging from the contract law to the tax law. It is our hope against hope that the private sector in India which has survived despite minimal opportunities, will finally get the recognition and encouragement from the State to contribute to India's space story.

---

8. Section 15 of the Commercial Space Launch Act, 1984 in the United States of America advocates a two tier approach where the outright sale of Government property is sought to be subjected to a fair market-value based approach whereas the other kinds of transfer like licenses are subjected to a "direct cost"-based approach.

9. See "Perspectives for a Comprehensive G.I. Policy (Including a National G.I. Policy Draft)", Mukund Rao and K.R. Sridhar Murthy, National institute of Advanced Studies, September, 2012.

10. See the Delhi Geographical Spatial Data Infrastructure (Management, Control, Administration, Safety and Security) Act, 2011.

11. Commercialisation and Privatisation of Outer Space: Exploiting the Commercial Value of Space

D. S. GOVINDRAJAN

Overview of Indian Space

In India, space activities were initiated in 1962, with the setting up of the Indian National Committee for Space Research (INCOSPAR). Initially, space research was conducted in India mainly with the help of sounding rockets. Space research activities acquired prominence with the establishment of the Indian Space Research Organisation (ISRO) in 1969 and the formation of the Space Commission and the Department of Space in 1972. India has effectively developed space technology and has applied it successfully for its rapid development and today is offering a variety of space services globally. One can describe the evolution of the Indian Space Programme as – 1970s: Era of Experimentation; 1980s: Era of Operationalisation.

During the operational phase in the 1990s, major space infrastructure was created under two broad classes: one for communication, broadcasting and meteorology through a multi-purpose Indian National Satellite system (INSAT) and the other for the Indian Remote Sensing Satellite (IRS) system. The development and operationalisation of the Polar Satellite Launch Vehicle (PSLV) and development of the Geosynchronous Satellite Launch Vehicle (GSLV) were significant achievements during this phase.

ISRO's long-term plan 'Vision 2025' for the Space Research Programme encompasses the development of reusable launch vehicles, human space flights, enhanced imaging capability, satellite based communication, navigation systems and planetary exploration.

ISRO has so far carried out 74 spacecraft missions and 45 launch missions and currently has a constellation of 9 communication satellites, 1 meteorological satellite, 10 earth observation satellites and 1 scientific satellite. Following are the highlights of ISRO:

- PSLV is a highly successful launch vehicle which has launched thirty spacecrafts into a variety of orbital paths so far;
- GSLV is an expendable launch system developed to enable India to launch its INSAT-type satellites into geostationary orbit;

- Mars Orbiter Mission is ISRO's first interplanetary mission to Mars. The Mars Orbiter Mission (MOM) from ISRO has recently completed its 100th orbit around the Red Planet, marking yet another milestone of the country's space efforts.

India now ranks among the top six spacefaring nations in the world in the terms of budget and technological capabilities. India's space budget accounts for approx. 0.14 per cent of the GDP. Almost half of the budget is focused on development and operation of launch vehicles and related activities. The remaining is devoted to space technology and applications including satellite operations.

Looking Ahead

It may be appropriate here to recall the words of the former President of India, (late) Dr. A.P.J. Abdul Kalam:

> *"Mankind's 21st century thrust into space would herald in the world's next industrial revolution, which might be called the 'Space Industrial Revolution'. This does not mean that the revolution will take place only in space; it essentially means the creation of architectural and revolutionary changes leading to new space markets, systems and technologies on a planetary scale."*

While what India is doing makes a lot of sense, this now needs to be converted into sound business sense. Hence, it is important to understand, review and analyse the commercial aspects that we are deliberating here. We must understand that while going to the Moon may not bring any commercial value, nevertheless it has a great impact on the economy.

Space offers enormous business opportunities and here, we must also realise that there is a shift from the nations to the commercial enterprises. Some of the examples being:

- Space X: A private spaceflight company which docked with the International Space Station in May 2012 and marked the beginning of this new era of commercial space race;
- Orbital Science: was the second private company to send a spacecraft to the space station;
- Many other firms including Virgin Galactic, Blue Origin and XCOR Aerospace are making their own rockets and then

- There are satellites such as Planet Labs, Skybox Imaging and Nanosatisfi, among other small firms which have taken on what was once the domain of the governments and big corporations.

What is also important to note is that:
- Students are also joining the space race: The Surrey University Space Centre, UK, blasted a rocket into orbit. Its payload: a smartphone kitted out to do some basic research.
- Generation Orbit (GO), a start-up based in Atlanta, is run by just a handful of young entrepreneurs/seasoned aerospace veterans and specialises in providing dedicated launch services to the emerging market for tiny nanosatellites.

The space industry still has untapped potential for major industrial growth. In order for the space industry to fulfil this potential, it must provide commercial returns; then it will be able to attract commercial capital investment.
- With more nations realising the strategic impact and economic potential of space, the motivations for a national space activity are not only about the fulfilment of ambitions but also about the development of an industry that can compete in a global marketplace.
- The global space industry has been experiencing a steady growth throughout—With the realisation of an economic potential in the space sector, there have been steady increases in both the space budgets by the governments and the spending by the commercial sector; the future prospects for generating value are promising.
- Investment in the Space Industry has produced good returns (i) Directly in the form of communications, remote sensing and many other capabilities and (ii) indirectly in the form of technological spin-offs, national prestige and scientific knowledge.

With so much of success in the space sector, India cannot afford to lag behind. India has to do a lot to efficiently utilise its resources and infrastructure and to implement a proper policy and programme for the commercialisation of its space sector.

Towards this end, the following suggestions are made:
- Explore "Make In India" Opportunities
  - *Effective use of infrastructure*

- o *Encourage public-private–partnerships*
- o *Exploit the rich talent pool and increase the operational efficiency*
- Encourage the Government-Industry-Academia Triad to enable a core indigenous competence in the critical areas
- Government or Industry-sponsored competitions to develop new applications.
- Create leadership programmes
- Fund for young entrepreneurs
  - o The fund should be independent of the Government and should encourage industry participation.
- Establish "Space Tech Park"
  - o On the lines of the Skolkovo Foundation, Harwell Space Cluster, EU Foundation, NASA Program
  - o Policy: address national security and industry requirements
  - o Ease of doing business: Quick and predictable responses and the Government should act more as a facilitator.

The above will definitely provide both short-term and long-term benefits to the country.

We must work towards diversifying the Indian economy through innovation and entrepreneurship. In this context, it may be worthwhile to look at a case study, which will clearly demonstrate as to how an innovation driven by competition provide better results.

Case Study: A $10M Competition to usher in a New Era of Private Space Travel

On October 4, 2004, SpaceShipOne made the second of two sub-orbital flights in one week, claiming the elusive Ansari X-Prize. Funded by the Ansari family, the Ansari X-Prize challenged teams from around the world to build a reliable, reusable, privately financed, manned spaceship capable of carrying three people to 100 km above the Earth's surface twice within two weeks. The prize was awarded in 2004 and along with it, a brand new private space industry was launched. The competition was launched in May 1996 and awarded on October 4, 2004. Altogether, 26 teams from 7 nations competed for the prize. The $10 million prize purse was awarded to the Mojave Aerospace Ventures team, led by the famed aerospace designer Burt Rutan and his company Scaled Composites, with financial backing from Paul Allen. The winning technology was licensed by Richard Branson to create Virgin Galactic and the prize competition itself launched a $2 billion private space industry.

To Conclude

- We must complement the success of India's space programme and understand that India has a significant ground to cover in order to address the major challenges and to grab the opportunities.
- Space offers plenty of Business Opportunities. It is all about enabling a new industry where we will be able to attract new talent and new investments, and see the technology transfer into other industries, and transform them.
- Space is an industry of the future, and we need to be ready to deal with it properly.
- The policy must provide lower barriers to entry which will attract more entrepreneurs enabling technological advancements and innovation leading to new applications.
- We need to focus on the mission to realise our vision and develop the human capital through research and provide value to partnerships. There is no better time than now to "Do It in a Better Way". The future is bright and let us make it right.

Brief Comments

1. Space Law in the Age of Privatisation and Commercialisation

SALIGRAM BHATT

Introduction

The NLSIU Bangalore has had a nice interactive conference on space law/ space legislation in India. Perhaps, the focus is on what the space law can be in the age of privatisation and commercialisation. Space law has followed space technology ever since the year 1957 when the space exploration began. It was the time when the States were engaged in the IGY programme—to know more about planet earth. It was the time for international cooperation between states. The former USSR took initiative to make a breakthrough in space exploration by the Soviet Sputnik. Even today, the USA borrows the ex-Soviet launch rockets for certain space exploits. India has gotten help in rocket science.

The jurists and scientists promoted ideas for law and order in space from the year 1957 onwards. Both the USA and the former Soviet Union held global conferences to produce perspectives on space law. The trend was for sharing the knowledge for the common benefits of humankind. The international law was based on the peaceful uses of space. Soon, the UN took over lawmaking by passing resolutions in the UNGA. Thus, the international law and the Charter of the UN was extended to the outer space. The Resolution on certain principles of space law was made into a declaration by the UN. A UN Committee for Peaceful Uses for Outer Space has been functioning from the early period of space exploration.

The second stage for space law started with the enactment of the Outer Space Treaty (OST) in 1967. It forms the charter of law for space exploration. Four more treaties/conventions followed the OST. These concerned the Rescue of Astronauts, the Liability Convention, the Registration Convention and the Agreement on the Moon made in 1979. The UN also produced five Declarations by the UNGA. Direct Television Broadcasts in 1982; the Remote Sensing of Earth from the Outer Space in 1986; the Use of Nuclear Power Sources in Space in 1992 and the International Cooperation Between the States for an Exploration and Use of Outer Space for the Benefits of all States, especially the Developing Countries, made in 1999.

Commercial uses and issues relating to privatisation: The world today is 58 years old in terms of space exploration. The space technology has improved tremendously with the landing on the Moon and the orbiting of Mars. More importantly, space exploration has made a revolution in communication, television, remote sensing of the earth and its natural resources, managing the biosphere with the new knowledge of science and space law. Space applications have made a new world order possible with more food production, new energy resources, forests and biodiversity management, new water management and rainwater and groundwater harvesting. A new earth science has come into being. The planet has become one large ecological unit, as we know today.

Besides the space science and technology, the world economy is already privatised. Private enterprise and market economy make the basis of trade and commerce between nations. We have the IMF, WTO, ITU, etc. making up the new reforms to change the old licence raj into a new creative economic world society. India in particular has adopted a new way of promoting the private economy into a competitive economy of a federal structure of states. Democracy, diversity and demand make up the market forces of the economy. The private enterprise has come into the forefront to help the public sector economy. We have a creative mixture of the private and public economic structure emerging. Let us see this economic image fitting into space exploration for the national economic benefits and for international cooperation.

The space legislation in India and its commercial uses and the privatisation economy go hand in hand. We have seen the global picture of the purpose of space law and of science. It is to promote the mutual economic benefits, to remove poverty and protect the environment by sustainable development. The Report of the UNISPACE III UN Conference 1999 has the title: "Space Exploration for the Benefits of Humanity in the 21st Century". A most apt title. I recommend you all to read this report that sums up also the benefits of space law and science, and secondly, the advantages of commercial uses and the privatisation of space activities.

Towards the end, we all want a space legislation in India for a harmonious development of the national economy and the safety and cooperation between the states. As said already, India is a party to five space treaties/agreements. India also is a party to six UN Declarations. Both of these categories give us the spirit of space law both for international and national uses. Many current laws from the Indian Constitution are being used to meet the needs of space legislation. India has a creative organisation to manage the national and international needs of space exploration. The purpose of space exploration and the national vision document was presented to the UNISPACE III conference in India 1999. It also gives brilliantly the uses of space application in many diverse fields of economy, natural resources, education and communication. The Department of Space along with the ISRO has held a national conference of the legal and scientific experts to draft a Space Act for India. The draft Act is to be approved by the Parliament. It is nice to reflect in brief that this draft Act has incorporated the aims and objectives of space exploration, has incorporated the essentials of the international space acts and declarations, has made good grounds for the entry of private enterprise to support the national efforts, has provided all clearances for the commercialisation of space exploration, has taken measures for the national safety and security, provided interaction with the concerned departments and stressed that India stands for the peaceful uses of space, poverty removal, international cooperation and environment protection. The draft Act is a shining work of law and science.

2.   Institutionalisation of Space Law in India

MALAY ADHIKARI

There is no disagreement from any corner that the private commercial activities require regulation. This regulation could be developed through policy, legislation and institution. Therefore the policy, legislation and institution—all are equally required to work out a national space legislation. The building-up of institutions for regulating space activities is one kind of soft regulation. Finally, these institutions play the pivotal role in making policies or legislations as prescribed later on. Another area of international law like the international environmental law has triggered the same strategy to regulate the environmental problems. This is known as the institutionalisation of environmental law.[1]

There are many countries like India that are in the highways of national space legislation. These countries have pursued the above strategy i.e. to regulate the space activities for the building up of distinct institutions. Sometimes, the countries promote the process of the development of national space legislation through the existing institutions that relate somehow to space activities.[2] One of them is Pakistan—India's immediate, but hostile, neighbour. Moreover, being one of the influential members of the SAARC countries, its space strategies must be observed and analysed in order to make successful the legal functioning of the SAARC satellite in the coming years. There is a trend towards a biennial national space conference under the umbrella of the national space agency, Pakistan Space and Upper Atmospheric Research Commission (SUPARCO). This conference was started in 2012. There have been sessions to develop the space law in Pakistan following the provisions of the international space law.[3] The legal sessions in the consecutive biennial conferences have made some soft regulations for evolving the future space legislation in the country. Alongside, the Research Society of International Law (RSIL), is another example of institutionalising the space law in Pakistan.[4] Their discussions over the space law guide on how to make a national space legislation.

The above example has been practiced in Africa. The continent has a programme like the African Leadership Conference on Space Science & Technology (ALC). It is also a biennial programme. It was started in 2005 but the space law session was introduced in 2007.[5] This programme is an institutional effort where the legal session is dedicated to the exchange of views amongst all the participating African countries' delegates to develop and promote a space law in the continent.

In this international background, an institutionalisation of the space law was indirectly commenced in India during 1955. It was the International Geophysical Year (IGY). This was the first national attempt to institutionalise the space activities for forming a national committee for the IGY.[6] This effort was carried forward later on through the setting up of the Indian Space Research Organization (ISRO), the Department of Space (DoS), the Space Commission and lastly, the ANTRIX Corporation in 1992.[7] All these were attempts to institutionalise the national space activities. But, these endeavours were made only for the state that was the prime actor in the space activities during this period.

This institutionalisation process has been shared by the private actors afterwards. Few examples are followed here. The Society of Indian Aerospace Technologies & Industries (SIATI) was established in 1991 to institutionalise the private actors in the aerospace industry. The ambit of the SIATI covers the issues regulating such actors.[8] Then, this institutionalising process was advanced through the Confederation of Indian Industries (CII) since 2008 by holding the Bengaluru Space Business Expo biennially through a devoted session on space law;[9] next is the Federation of Indian Chambers of Commerce & Industry (FICCI) since 2008, but focused on geospatial regulation;[10] next is the Association of Geospatial Industries (AGI) since 2008 again on geospatial regulation;[11] last but not the least, is the Cellular Operators Association of India (COAI) since 1995 focused on the telecommunication regulations.[12]

There are other institutions in India that are directly and indirectly engaged with the promotion of space activities.[13] All their deliberations and representations make the soft regulations (direct/indirect) for the space activities that have been part of the process of the national space legislation movement for a decade or more. These institutional contributions including the process of the foundation of such organisations are not less significant than regulating the national space activities through policies and legislations.

In conclusion, there should be some provision for institutionalising the space law within the upcoming 'Space Act' which has been prescribed in the 12th Five Year Plan (2012–2017).[14] Before that, there must be strong initiative to develop more institutions or associations or a consortium of institutions concerned with the national space activities. Within such organisations, there would be a requirement for an innovative, optimistic (i.e. not criticising the government's space infrastructure always) and an interdisciplinary exchange of ideas and thoughts. It will not definitely be a substitute for the upcoming 'Space Act' but may play the role of a legal standby for the time being.

References:
1. Desai, B. H. (2004), *Institutionalizing International Environmental Law*, New York: Transnational Publishers.
2. Space Programmes of China, Japan, the Republic of Korea, UAE, etc.
3. Pakistan Space and Upper Atmospheric Research Commission website.
4. http://rsilpak.org/(Accessed on 25 July, 2015).
5. Martinez, P. (2012), "The African Leadership Conference on Space Science and Technology for Sustainable Development", *Space Policy*, 28(1), pp. 33-37.
6. Kochar, R. (2008), "Science as a Symbol of New Nationhood: India and the International Geophysical Year 1957-58", *Current Science*, 94(6), pp. 813-816.
7. ISRO website.
8. http://www.siati.org/ (Accessed on 25 July, 2015).
9. http://www.bsxindia.com/index.asp (Accessed on 25 July, 2015).
10. http://www.ficci.com/sector-overview.asp?secid=85 (Accessed on 25July, 2015)
11. http://agiindia.com/about-us/objectives/;http://agiindia.com/what-we-do/advisory-initiatives/ (Accessed on 26July, 2015).
12. http://www.coai.com/About-Us/About-COAI (Accessed on 26July, 2015).
13. Adhikari, M. (2014), "Developing Space Law Education in India: Some Proposals", *Rostrum's Law Review*, I (4). http://rostrumlegal.com/blog/developing-space-law-education-in-india-some-proposals-by-malay-adhikari/ (Accessed on 26July 2015).
14. http://planningcommission.nic.in/aboutus/committee/wrkgrp12/sandt/wg_dos2905.pdf (Accessed on 26July, 2015).

3. The Private Space Activity Regulator's Role in the Space Environment Protection: A Policy Snapshot

DEVA PRASAD M.

The private space activities' regulator (henceforth "Regulator/regulator") has an important role to play in the case of space environment protection. In the Indian context, the proposed national space legislation is a tool, which could provide clarity regarding the role of the regulator.

This note tries to emphasise the need for the regulator to ensure protection of the space environment. Space debris is a pertinent problem to be tackled, which poses a risk to the outer space activities. The space debris, which could be understood as non-functional manmade space objects, is polluting the outer space environment. The existence of space debris primarily causes a risk of collision to satellites and the space station.

In this context, space debris mitigation should be an important agenda for the regulator. The private space activity, which leads to the creation of the space debris above a particular threshold, should be regulated. The international space law framework does not mandate any particular guideline for regulating the private space activities. Even the Liability Convention 1972 is not equipped to regulate the private space activities and their impact upon the outer space environment.

The existence of a well-evolved legal framework of the Earthly environmental protection measure in India could be relied upon for drawing a parallel analogy. For example, the well-established Polluter Pay Principle (PPP) could be applied in those situations where the private space activity leads to a creation of the space debris above a particular threshold. By applying the Polluter Pay Principle, the regulator would be equipped with a tool to control the unwanted private space activities.

Another important tool for the regulator is the Environmental Impact Assessment (EIA) mechanism. A possible impact on the outer space environment could be analysed from an ex-ante perspective using the EIA mechanism. The 'ILA Draft Model Law on National Space Legislation' also emphasises the need for an EIA mechanism for the purpose of the protection of the outer space environment. Article 7, paragraph 2, of the 'ILA Draft

Model Law on National Space Legislation' states: "An environmental impact assessment is required before the beginning of a space activity". Apart from the Polluter Pay Principle and the EIA mechanism, other significant environmental law principles and concepts such as the precautionary principle and the sustainable development concept could be made applicable for the purpose of the outer space environmental protection.

India's national space legislation should provide the regulator with a sufficient power to invoke and apply the significant environmental protection principles as mentioned above in the context of the private space activities. India, as a spacefaring country having a long-term interest in the outer space activities would have to ensure that the outer space environment is kept stable for exploration. The regulator would have to look into the public interest element of India's long-term interest in outer space. India's national space legislation should contain provisions protecting India's interest in the outer space.

Moreover, the regulator also should take into account futuristic activities such as the outer space natural resource exploitation and space tourism. These are activities, which would have a serious outer space environmental impact in the future. Further, the private space actors would also be keen to engage in these activities. Hence, the national space legislation should enable the regulator to look into the future issues affecting the outer space environment. Here also, the established principles of the environmental law would be beneficial in dealing with the various issues.

Further, in the case of proposed space activities such as space tourism, the safety of the human participants in those activities also needs to be considered. The regulator should also be enabled in order to devise a policy for the safety of such space activities. The application of the risk management principles such as a precautionary principle would be beneficial in such situations.

The national space legislation should equip the regulator to devise policies and regulations in these areas for the purpose of controlling the private space actors. The private space actors should be regulated in order to ensure that they do not adversely impact the outer space environment. This brief note has just flagged the agenda that the private space regulator would have to engage in. The national space legislation would have to address these concerns seriously.

4. Need for a Business Incubation in the Indian Space Programme

PRATEEP BASU

India's space industry primary stakeholder is the government, and it has remained so ever since the inception of the national space programme due to the lack of volumes in the industry. Efforts have been made in the past to bring together the industry giants to form a consortium and undertake the commercial space activities, but all such efforts have been unsuccessful due to the lack of a domestic market. The global market for space technology products and services is highly oligopolistic, with a few big firms having excellent capabilities and a high degree of the market share. An industry cannot be created based purely on the external demands for the goods and services, and such demand for space-based services has to be generated internally. The establishment of a business incubator could potentially achieve that by creating new markets and making access to the global markets easier; paving the way for a greater involvement of the bigger players for upstream activities like satellite manufacturing and launch services.

The successes of Chandrayaan-1 and Mangalyaan have buoyed the ISRO to outsource more high-end work to private companies, and the commercial aerospace industry is now eager to play a larger role in the space missions and to tap the outsourcing work offered by the ISRO. The government's recent announcement to dedicate funds up to INR 10,000 Cr (~$1.5 billion) for start-ups by entrepreneurs through different channels has elated the mood of the entrepreneurs and the investors alike. It is therefore the right time for the ISRO to consider setting up a 'Business Incubator' that could encourage the entrepreneurs to take up business ideas that apply space technology to non-space industrial, scientific and commercial fields. Such an initiative would increase the rate at which the technology is transferred; create a competitive value-added domestic products industry; contribute to economic and industrial growth of the nation and provide an additional branding for the ISRO among the youth.

The European Space Agency (ESA) and the UK Space agency have adopted such a approach to facilitate the formation of a strong downstream space services industry. The ESA has created an annual fund called the 'Open Sky Technology Fund' of €100 million for supporting start-ups that make use of the ESA's technology (ESA, 2014). The fund is managed by a VC firm called Triangle Ventures. The ESA BIC programme has succeeded in creating around 50 viable companies till date and serves as a good model for the space agencies to encourage entrepreneurship. The UK Space Agency organises annual business-plan events in collaboration with the domestic aerospace industry by giving need-based problem statements and inviting the business ideas around them. The top teams are selected for incubation at their Harwell space cluster and provided a financial and mentoring support to establish their product and to sell it profitably. Spin-offs and technology transfer policies have been framed eloquently by these space agencies to reap the tangible and intangible benefits of space technology by involving entrepreneurs who are willing to take risks.

These steps are helping these space agencies leverage their core competencies and gain a competitive advantage over other nations because of the presence of a robust SME sector supporting the space programme. Such policy mechanisms allow the space agencies to make the shift from being efficiency-driven organisations to being innovation-driven organisations. Along the lines of the ESA's 'Open Sky Technology Fund', a dedicated fund vehicle must be created by the ISRO and the DOS solely for the purpose of providing seed money to the early-stage startups whose business plans revolve around the space technology-based products and services. A public–private partnership between Antrix and a Venture Capital (VC) firm can be set up that shall operate under the Space Commission and manage the funds on behalf of the ISRO. Their primary responsibility shall be to take up the consideration for the independent business proposals on a quarterly basis. The selection panel shall have the relevant technology experts from the ISRO, while the financial and markets aspects shall be vetted by Antrix and the VC firm. The involvement of a VC firm is necessary to streamline the process of selection of business plans with good market potential and providing a sound financial advice to the entrepreneurs during the course of incubation.

Thus, India and ISRO need to act quickly to tap the innovation potential of India's entrepreneurs and play the mentor for creating a service-based industry that can assist the ISRO in fulfilling the goals of the national space programme.

Annexures

1.   The ILA Model Law

STEPHAN HOBE

Presentation

by

Prof Dr Stephan Hobe, LLM
Director of the Institute of Air and Space Law
University of Cologne, Germany

§ 13 Principles and Examples of National Space Legislation

**Model Law for National Space Legislation
Second Reading
by Prof Dr Stephan Hobe
(Rapporteur of the ILA Space Law Committee)**
The author acknowledges the contributions of Joanne Gabrynowicz, Irmgard Marboe, Frank Maes, Tanja Masson-Zwaan, Matxalen Sanchez, and Kai-Uwe Schrogl.

In view of the discussion of the Space Law Committee of the International Law Association held at the 74th Biannual Conference in The Hague, the following revised version of a model law for a special space legislation is hereby proposed:

1. General Remarks
In the view of this Rapporteur, there are indispensable requirements underlying any future model law, as follows:
- Duty and details for authorisation procedures and licensing, and respective requirements,
- Duty of supervision,
- Necessary insurance for private space actors.

§ 13 Principles and Examples of National Space Legislation

In the Workshop on the National Space Legislation which was held in 2004 in the framework of the Project 2001 Plus as a cooperation exercise between the Cologne Institute of Air and Space Law and the German Aerospace Center (DLR), a number of the so-called 'building-blocks' for national space laws were adopted. Those building blocks were considered crucial in that they should be addressed by any kind of national space law. Among those building blocks were:

1. Authorisation of space activities,

2. Supervision of space activities,

3. Registration of space objects,

4. Compensation, regulation and

5. Additional regulation.[1]

§ 13 Principles and Examples of National Space Legislation

Thus, the basis was laid down by the major findings of the Project 2001 Plus and in particular its Workshop on National Space Legislation. Moreover, further doctrinal discussion is appropriately recorded in the commentary to Article VI of the Outer Space Treaty in Stephan Hobe, Bernhard Schmidt-Tedd and Kai-Uwe Schrogl (eds.), *Cologne Commentary on Space Law*, Cologne 2009, pp. 103-125 (by Michael Gerhard) and the various national space laws of earlier as well as of a more recent nature. The following proposal of a Model Law should be seen as a guideline and source for further discussion. It attempts to integrate the doctrinal approaches as well as practical needs.

§ 13 Principles and Examples of National Space Legislation

2. The Proposed Model Law on National Space Legislation

Article 1- Scope of application

The present law applies to the space activities carried out by the citizens of XY or by the legal persons incorporated in XY and the space activities carried out within the territory of XY or on the ships or aircrafts registered in XY.

Comment:

This provision shall, at the beginning, clarify the scope of regulation for the national space law on the human activities in outer space. It should be clear that a specific (genuine) link should exist for the respective country which enacts the specific law. This link could be either the nationality of the natural or the legal person involved in the carrying out of activities in a certain territory on the national register for ships and aircrafts. The latter is important with regard to the space activities on the High Seas.

In the following, 'XY' will be used to denote the respective state enacting the national space legislation on the basis of the present Model Law.

§ 13 Principles and Examples of National Space Legislation

Article 2 – Definitions – Use of Terms

The following definitions will apply for the purposes of this law:

Space activity: The term 'space activity' includes the launch, operation, guidance, and re-entry of space objects into, in and from outer space and other activities essential for the launch, operation, guidance and re-entry of space objects into, in and from outer space.

Space object: The term 'space object' refers to any object launched or intended to be launched into outer space including its component parts as well as its launch vehicle and the parts thereof.

Operator: The term 'operator' refers to a natural or legal person carrying out the space activities.

Authorisation: License delivered in written form.

Supervision: Continuous observation and tracking of a space activity.

Commercial space activity: A space activity for the purpose of generating revenue or profit whether conducted by a governmental or by a non-governmental entity.

§ 13 Principles and Examples of National Space Legislation

Comment:

The definition of "space activity" is in line with the current international space law and state practice.

Arguably, one could add that activities at an altitude of 100 km above sea level are considered space activities.

The definition of "space object" reflects the current state practice and includes the official definition given in the Registration and in the Liability Conventions (See also Kerrest, Smith, in Hobe, Schmidt-Tedd and Schrogl (eds.), *Cologne Commentary on Space Law*, Vol. 1, p. 140.)

Authorisation and supervision shall be based on the Outer Space Treaty and the current State practice.

N.B. This list is not exhaustive. National legislators are free to add more definitions if they consider them necessary.

§ 13 Principles and Examples of National Space Legislation

Article 3: Authorisation

All space activities are subject to authorisation. Authorisation shall be granted by the minister of … (= the competent minister).

Comment:

The Article lays down the fundamental obligation under Article VI, the second sentence of the Outer Space Treaty, namely that all the national space activities need to be licensed. For this reason, a respective licensing authority is to be either established or, alternatively, an existing authority may be established as the licensing authority.

Authorisation may take several forms ranging from general licenses to individual licenses or permits.

§ 13 Principles and Examples of National Space Legislation

Article 4: Conditions for Authorisation

(1) Authorisation shall be granted if the following conditions are met:
(a) The operator is in a financial position to undertake space activities,
(b) The operator has proven to be reliable and to has the required technical knowledge,
(c) The space activity does not cause any environmental damage to the Earth and outer space in accordance with Article 7,
(d) The space activity mitigates space debris in accordance with Article 8,
(e) The space activity is compliant with public safety standards,
(f) The space activity does not run counter to national security interests,
(g) The space activity does not run counter to the international obligations and foreign policy interests of XY,
(h) The operator has complied with the ITU Regulations with regard to frequency allocations and orbital positions,
(i) The operator complies with insurance requirements as determined in Article 12.
(2) In order to prove the fulfilment of the conditions mentioned in paragraph (1), the operator must submit the appropriate documentation and evidence (as specified in an implementing decree/regulation).
(3) The authorisation may contain conditions and requirements.

§ 13 Principles and Examples of National Space Legislation

Comment:

It must be made sure that the applicant is personally reliable and in a secure financial position. Moreover, the requirements of foreign policy, national security, public safety, international telecommunication regulations and insurance should be fulfilled. A written documentation gives proof of these facts.

Article 5: Supervision: All space activities are subject to continuous supervision by the minister. Details of this supervision shall be laid down in an implementing decree/regulation.

Comment:

Supervision is the other requirement mentioned in Article VI, sentence 2 of the Outer Space Treaty. It shall be undertaken by the same authority responsible for the licensing. Furthermore, it should be made sure that such an information is available at the government level.

Article 6: Withdrawal, Suspension or Amendment of Authorisation: The minister may withdraw, suspend or amend the authorisation, if the conditions of Article 4 para. 1 or the specific conditions or requirements of Article 4 para. 3 are not complied with.

Comment:

Withdrawal, suspension and amendment should be the usual forms of supervision of the authorising minister, notwithstanding the additional sanctions contained in Article 14.

§ 13 Principles and Examples of National Space Legislation

Article 7: Protection of the Environment

(1) The space activities shall not cause any environmental damage to the Earth and outer space or parts of it, directly or indirectly.

(2) An environmental impact assessment is required before the beginning of a space activity.

(3) Details of the environmental impact assessment shall be laid down in an implementing decree/regulation.

Comment:

In order to ensure that the space activities undertaken by private actors meet the highest environmental standards, an environmental impact assessment must be carried out. See also the Cosmic Study of the International Academy of Astronautics on the Protection of the Environment of Celestial Bodies of the year 2010 which includes similar recommendations.

§ 13 Principles and Examples of National Space Legislation

Article 8: Mitigation of Space Debris

(1) Space activities shall be carried out in such a manner as to mitigate to the greatest possible extent any potential space debris in accordance with Article 4(d).

(2) The obligation of para. 1 includes the obligation to limit the debris released during normal operations, to minimise the potential for on-orbit break-ups, to prepare for post-mission disposal and to prevent on-orbit collisions in accordance with the international space debris mitigation standards.

Comment:

In view of the recent discussion on the mitigation of space debris, all efforts should be made to mitigate the space debris. The obligations mentioned in para. 2 refer to international standards and guidelines on space debris mitigation. The competent national authorities should make sure that the operators comply with these international standards and guidelines, such as the IADC Space Debris Mitigation Guidelines or the UN COPUOS Space Debris Mitigation Guidelines.

§ 13 Principles and Examples of National Space Legislation

Article 9: Transfer of space activity: The transfer of a space activity to another operator is subject to a prior authorisation by the minister. Authorisation will be granted under the conditions of Article 4.

Comment:

Any transfer of space activity to another operator may cause additional problems. It must be made sure that the new operator fulfils the same conditions for conducting the respective space activity as mentioned in Article 4. Therefore, any such transfer of a space activity needs to have the authorisation of the competent minister.

In-orbit transfers of ownership or transfer and control of a space object are also included in this article.

§ 13 Principles and Examples of National Space Legislation

Article 10: Registration

(1) A national register is hereby established for the registration of space objects. The minister of ... (= competent minister, preferably the same as in Article 3) keeps the national space register.

(2) Subject to paragraph 3 of this article, all the space objects for which XY is the launching state according to Article 1 of the Convention on Registration of Objects Launched into Outer Space of 1974, shall be registered in the national register.

(3) If there are two or more launching States in respect of any such space object, the agreement among them according to Article II para. 2 of the International Convention on the Registration of Objects Launched into Outer Space shall be determinative of the registration in XY.

(4) The following information has to be entered into the national register:
- Name of the launching state or states (name of a private launching entity: natural or legal person),
- Registration number of the space object,
- Date and territory or location of the launch,
- Basic orbital parameters including nodal period, inclination, apogee, perigee,
- General function of the space object.

§ 13 Principles and Examples of National Space Legislation

Article 10: Registration

(5) Additional information and information in accordance with the Registration Convention and/or the UN Registration Practice Resolution as specified in an implementing decree/regulation shall also be included in the national register.

(6) The information contained in para. 1 shall be made available to the Secretary-General of the United Nations as soon as possible.

(7) Any relevant change with regard to the information mentioned in para. 1 must be registered in the national register. The Secretary-General of the United Nations shall be informed accordingly.

Comment:

In order to comply with the obligation to inform the United Nations about the space activities and to register the space objects, the states need to get the respective information from the operators. Therefore, the establishment of a national register and the obligation of the operators to produce this information put the state in the position to fulfil its international obligations.

§ 13 Principles and Examples of National Space Legislation

Article 11: Liability and Recourse

(1) When XY has paid compensation to the third parties for the damage caused by a space activity in fulfilment of its international obligations, the government is entitled to take recourse against the operator.

(2) The recourse of the government against the operator may be limited to a certain amount.

Comment:

If the state is liable under the Liability Convention or under general international law to pay compensation to third parties, the government may want to have recourse against the operator. The amount of such recourse may be limited.

In some legislations, it might be necessary to establish the operator's liability separately. Otherwise, the right of recourse would not have a legal basis. This is particularly true for the liability without fault.

§ 13 Principles and Examples of National Space Legislation

Article 11: Liability and Recourse

Comment:

Therefore, an additional "Article 11a" could be inserted which could read:

"(1) The operator is absolutely liable to pay compensation for the damage caused by a space object on the surface of the earth or on an aircraft in flight.

(2) For a damage caused elsewhere, the operator is liable only if the damage is due to its fault or the fault of persons for whom it is responsible.

(3) The liability according to para. (1) is limited to ### (to be decided, i.e. either insurable sum or fixed amount)."

The advantage of such a provision is that the liability of the operator is established which can also be brought before national courts. The injured parties therefore do not need to go through diplomatic channels as foreseen in the Liability Convention but can enforce their claims in private litigation, which of course is preferable to the state and also to the victims.

§ 13 Principles and Examples of National Space Legislation

In case of fault liability, the operator will anyway be liable for damage on the basis of the ordinary tort law. Usually, there is no ceiling for such a liability under the national law.

However, absolute liability must have a ceiling in most legislations. So, the national legislator might need to think about such a ceiling. This ceiling could either reflect the amount which can reasonably be insured or be a fixed sum. State practice shows various models. The ceiling usually corresponds to the ceiling foreseen with regard to the right of recourse in Article 7 para. 2.

The ceiling of the liability of the operator does, of course, not change the liability of the state which remains absolute and unlimited for the damage caused to the third parties on the surface of the Earth or to the aircraft in flight.

§ 13 Principles and Examples of National Space Legislation

Article 12: Insurance

(1) The operator carrying out a space activity shall be insured to cover the damage caused to the third parties up to the amount of... (to be established by national law).

(2) The obligation of para. 1 does not apply if the government itself carries out the space activity.

(3) The minister may waive the obligation to insure if

a) the operator has a sufficient equity capital to cover the amount of his/her liability;

b) the space activity is not a commercial space activity and is in the public interest.

(4) The details of the content and the conditions of the insurance shall be laid down in an implementing decree/regulation.

Comment:

The obligation of insurance has two reasons: firstly, the operator must insure himself/herself for fault (and, in accordance with the proposed Article 11a) also absolute liability. This is advisable as the space activities are inherently dangerous and can have catastrophic consequences. Secondly, it renders it more realistic that the state can effectively exercise its right of recourse based on Article 11.

The amount of insurance may be established according to different criteria (C.f. Section 3 (4) of the Dutch Space Activities Act which subjects it to "what can reasonably be covered by insurance", and Art 6 (I) of the French Space Operations Act which requires insurance up to the liability cap.) Some harmonisation of the required amount of insurance should be aimed at because otherwise there could be a danger of license shopping. The Model Law or the comment could, therefore, contain some guidance for possible limits.

§ 13 Principles and Examples of National Space Legislation

Article 13: Procedure

(1) The rules of procedure follow the general rules of (administrative) procedural law. This includes the time limits for the decision of the minister and the right to impose conditions and sanctions.

(2) Appropriate costs and tariffs for the procedure are laid down by the minister in the implementing decree/regulation.

(3) Any dispute arising from the interpretation and/or application of the present law shall be resolved within the national jurisdiction or by agreement under the New Rules of the Permanent Court of Arbitration for Arbitration of Disputes relating to Outer Space Activities (2011).

Comment:

Disputes possibly arising from this Model Law should basically be judged upon in the national court system. They are not a matter for arbitration because, for e.g., the requirements of license or the fulfilment of the duty of supervision is actually not at the discretion of the parties involved. Therefore, a kind of duty stemming from these rules does not seem appropriate for arbitration.

§ 13 Principles and Examples of National Space Legislation

Article 14: Sanctions

A violation of the obligations set out by the present law is punishable by a fine of ##.####. The carrying out of space activities and the transfer of space activities without authorisation by the minister according to Articles 3 and 9 is punishable at least by an amount of #.###.

Comment:

The law could, at this stage, establish an amount for the fine. It may also establish a criterion or make reference to an implementing decree/other national legislation. Reference may also be taken in light of the example of the French Operations Act.

Sentence 2 imposes a minimum sanction in the case of space activities and their transfer without a license. This is justified because of the gravity of the offence. The upper limit should be set at a deterring amount available for the violations of the administrative law; however, not reaching the level of a criminal sanction.

2. A National Space Law for India: Deconstructing the Proposition

RANJANA KAUL

NATIONAL SPACE LAW FOR INDIA

DECONSTRUCTING THE PROPOSITION

Ranjana Kaul

Commercialisation and Privatisation of Outer Space

Issues of National Space Legislation

Roundtable Conference
National Law School of India University, Bangalore
18 July, 2015

The Constitution of India
justice, liberty, equality, fraternity

Our Activities in Outer Space

- Harmonising the international obligations arising from the international treaties ratified by India through domestic law for the purpose of implementing the treaty obligations .

- National industrial/commercial activity for producing goods and services related to the access to and for space.

- < downstream aspects: upstream aspects>

India:
Engagement with the International Space Law Treaties

- Charter of the United Nations   Ratified
- 1967 Outer Space Treaty: Ratified 18/1/1982
- 1968 Rescue Agreement: Acceded 9/7/1979
- 1972 Liability Convention: Acceded 9/7/1979
- 1974 Registration Convention: Acceded 18/1/1982

- 1979 Moon Agreement: Signatory 18/1/1982

Ref: UN Glossary of terms relating to Treaty actions

1969 Vienna Convention on Law of Treaties *(came into force 1980)*

(consent to be bound)

International Law & the Outer Space Treaty

OST, Article III:

States Parties to the Treaty **shall carry on activities** in the exploration and use of outer space, including the Moon and other celestial bodies, **in accordance with international law, including the Charter of the United Nations,** in the interest of maintaining international peace and security and promoting international cooperation and understanding.

UN Charter, Article 2 (2):

All Members, in order to ensure to all of them the rights and benefits resulting from membership, **shall fulfil in good faith the obligations assumed by them in accordance with the present Charter.**

1969 Vienna Convention on Law of Treaties , Article 26

International Obligations
qua Domestic Law

Constitution

Article 51 :

1. Promotion of international peace and security;
2. Maintaining just and honourable relations;
3. Fostering respect for international law and treaty obligations;
4. Encourage settlement of international disputes by arbitration

Exceptions to Article 51:

1. Payment to a foreign power to be withdrawn from the Consolidated Fund of India;
2. Affects the justiciable rights of a citizen;
3. Requires the taking of private property [Art.31(1)], taking of life or liberty [Art.21], such as extradition or imposition of a tax [Art.265], which under the Constitution can be done only by legislation;
4. Modifies the laws of the State.

International Obligations
State Practice

Constitution

Article 53:

Empowers the President of India to exercise the executive power of the Union of India in accordance with the Constitution.

Article 73 (1):

The Executive Power of the Union shall extend to the exercise of such rights, authority and jurisdiction as are exercisable by the Government of India by virtue of any treaty or agreement:

****

* International treaties do not have the force of municipal law without appropriate legislation.

* Indian Courts are bound to give effect to the Indian law if there is a law to the contrary or an absence of the domestic law.

National Space Programme

- Prime Minister

- Space Commission

- Department of Space

- ISRO
- Centres, agencies, etc.

Constitution

- *Conduct of Government Business*

- **Article 77**: (1) **All executive action** of the Government of India shall be expressed to be taken **in the name of the President.**

- .....

- (3) **The President shall make rules** for the more convenient transaction of the business of the Government of India, and for the allocation among Ministers of the said business.

Constitution

Conduct of Government Business

Constitution Article13:

"......

(3) In this article, unless the context otherwise requires,—

(*a*) **"*law*" includes** any Ordinance, order, bye-law, rule, regulation, **notification**, custom or usage having in the territory of India the force of law; ....."

The Government of India (Allocation of Business) Rules, 1961
(as amended).

In exercise of the powers conferred by clause (3) of article 77 of the Constitution and in supercession of all previous rules and orders on the subject, the President hereby makes the following rules for the allocation of the business of the Government of India.

1. Short Title: These rules may be called the Government of India (Allocation of Business) Rules, 1961.

2. Allocation of Business: The business of the Government of India shall be transacted in the Ministries, Departments, Secretariats and Offices specified in the First Schedule to these rules (all of which are hereinafter referred to as "departments").

Framework for the Conduct of the National Space Activities

The Government of India (Allocation of Business) Rules, 1961
(as amended)

▪ **[45.] DEPARTMENT OF SPACE (ANTARIKSH VIBHAG)**

▪ **3. Distribution**

1. Space Commission and all matters relating thereto.

2. All matters relating to Space Science, Space Technology and Space Applications, including
(a) Research (including fundamental research) in matters connected with space and the development of its uses;
(b) all matters connected with Space Technology;
(c) all matters connected with Space Applications; and

Framework for the Conduct of Space Activities
The Government of India (Allocation of Business) Rules, 1961
(as amended)

▪ (d) all activities connected with the development and use of outer Space, including:

▪ (i) projects and industries connected with the utilisation of outer Space including the commercial exploitation of Space;

▪ (ii) Establishment, procurement and use of Space-based systems;

▪ (iii) the design, manufacture and launching of Rockets and Satellites; and

▪ (iv) work connected with Space Applications.

Framework for the Conduct of Space Activities
The Government of India (Allocation of Business) Rules, 1961
(as amended)

3. Financial Assistance for the furtherance of research and study in Space Science, Space Technology and Space Applications and for building up the adequate trained manpower for the development of the Space Programme including:

(a) assistance to institutions and associations engaged in scientific work and to Universities for advanced study and to Universities for advanced study and research in Space Science, Space Technology and Space Applications;

(b) grant of Scholarships to students in educational institutions, and other forms of financial aid to individuals including those going abroad for studies in the field of Space Science, Space Technology and Space Applications.

Framework for the Conduct of Space Activities
The Government of India (Allocation of Business) Rules, 1961
(as amended)

4. International relations in matters connected with Space, including:
(a) matters relating to Space in the United Nations specialised agencies and in relations with the other countries; and
(b) correspondence with Universities and other educational institutions abroad in connection with foreign scholarships and the training of Indian scientists.

5. All matters relating to the personnel under the control of the Department.
6. Execution of works and purchase of lands debit-able to the budget of the Department of Space.
7. Procurement of stores and equipment required by the Department of Space.
8. Financial sanctions relating to the Department of Space.

Framework for the Conduct of Space Activities
The Government of India (Allocation of Business) Rules, 1961
(as amended)

9. All matters relating to the Physical Research Laboratory, Ahmedabad.

10. All matters relating to National Remote Sensing Agency (NRSA).

11. All matters relating to the National Natural Resources Management System including the generation of integrated data mainly based on remote sensing and assistance in the analysis and dissemination of such information.

12. All matters relating to the National Mesosphere, Stratosphere and Troposphere Radar Facility (NMRF).

13. Antrix Corporation Limited.

14. North Eastern Space Applications Centre.

15. All matters relating to the Semiconductor Complex Limited (SCL), Mohali

Commercialising Space

- *DOS/ISRO Website*

- **The Indian space programme is guided by** the Allocation of Business Rules for the Department of Space, along with the related

- legislations and regulations of the Government of India and

- **Policies** such as:

- *Remote Sensing Data Policy:* under challenge in HC Delhi
- *Satcom Policy*
- Mapping Policy, etc.
    - *FDI Policy on private satellite systems (74% FDI)?*

New Telecom Policy, 1999
Commercialising Space

DOT: Wireless Planning Wing (Ministry Communications)

3.9 SATCOM Policy

The SATCOM Policy shall provide for users to avail the transponder capacity from both domestic /foreign satellites. However, the same has to be in consultation with the Department of Space.

Under the existing ISP policy, international long distance communication for data has been opened up. The gateways for this purpose shall be allowed to use SATCOM.

It has also been decided that the Ku frequency band shall be allowed to be used for communication purposes.

Procedure

* INSAT Coordination Committee (ICC): allotment of transponder capacity

Commercialising Space

PSLV: July 10, 2015

- The PSLV flight carries only commercial, non-Indian payloads.
- At US$ 33.3 m. per launch, the PSLV is a bargain given today's competition.

- The launch placed five satellites built by Surrey Satellite Technology Ltd. (SSTL) of Britain into a polar orbit.

- The main payload was the three-satellite DMC3 constellation of 1-meter-resolution spacecraft for Twenty-First Century Aerospace Technology Co., Beijing, which has purchased the entire capacity on the DMC3 constellation for seven years.

Going Forward ...
▣ Digital India & Make in/for India

▣ Absence of assured, high speed, low cost connectivity throughout the country will make it impossible to achieve Prime Minister Modi's "Digital India" target.

▣ *Indian NewSpace* offers potential to connect the entire country with innovative technologies for low cost, high speed, assured internet access at disruptive price points [Small Sats/launch vehicles/LEO].

▣ Simultaneously leap-frog India into the *new space economy*.
****

▣ Amend the GoI Allocation of Business Rules for the DOS in order to enable engagement.

▣ Rules/ procedures, applicable to both parties, must be issued under the proper authority and duly notified

▣ Thank you

3.   The Bangalore Declaration

National Law School of India University, Bangalore
&
TMT Law Practice, New Delhi
Round table conference on
"Commercialization and Privatization of Outer Space: Issues for National Space Legislation"
DATE: 18TH JULY 2015
VENUE: ALLEN & OVERY CONFERENCE HALL, 2ND FLOOR, TRAINING CENTRE, NLSIU,
BANGALORE

MEDIA PARTNER
WITNESS
INDIA'S FIRST MAGAZINE ON LEGAL
AND CORPORATE AFFAIRS

THE BANGALORE DECLARATION

Whereas with increasing commercialisation and privatisation in outer space several legal issues are likely,

Realising safety and security of India is of topmost priority,

Knowing compliance with International obligations and Constitutional obligations is non-derogable,

Recognising the fundamental need to encourage investors in outer space,

Appreciating the dire need for 'Rule of Law' in Outer Space,

Therefore this round table conference on COMMERCIALIZATION AND PRIVATIZATION OF SPACE: ISSUES FOR NATIONAL SPACE LEGISLATION held on 18TH JULY 2015 foresees the National Space Act for India as the enabler of space commerce and proclaims this document as **the Bangalore Declaration**. The National Space Act for India must minimally address the following issues:

1. Space Governance.
2. Licensing conditions.
3. Monitoring of space activities.
4. Liability for damages.
5. Protection of environment of space.
6. Registration of space objects.
7. Indemnification factors.
8. Insurance coverage.
9. Trade related aspects: sale/ transfer of space objects.
10. Research and development.
11. Data protection & IPR.
12. Technology transfer.
13. Sanctions for breach.
14. Dispute resolution.

4.   The Conference Programme Schedule

National Law School of India University, Bangalore
&
TMT Law Practice, New Delhi
Round table conference on
"Commercialization and Privatization of Outer Space: Issues for National Space Legislation"
DATE: 18TH JULY 2015

VENUE: ALLEN & OVERY CONFERENCE HALL, 2ND FLOOR, TRAINING CENTRE, NLSIU, BANGALORE

PROGRAMME SCHEDULE

MEDIA PARTNER
WITNESS
INDIA'S FIRST MAGAZINE ON LEGAL AND CORPORATE AFFAIRS
www.witnesslive.in

INAUGURAL SESSION 9:30 AM – 10:45 AM	
Invocation	**Students NLSIU B'lore.**
Welcome Address and about the Law School	**Prof. (Dr.) R. Venkata Rao** Vice-Chancellor, NLSIU B'lore.
About TMT Law Practice	**Mr. Abhishek Malhotra** Managing Partner, TMT Law Practice, New Delhi.
About the Conference	**Mr. Kumar Abhijeet** Assistant Professor, NLSIU B'lore, Conference Coordinator.
Key Note Address by the Chief Guest	**Hon'ble (Dr.) G. Madhavan Nair** President of the International Academy of Astronautics (IAA) and Former Chairman of the Indian Space Research Organization (ISRO).
Vote of Thanks	**Ms. Ashrutha Rai** Final Year Student, Space Law Course.
GROUP PHOTO **Tea Break: 10:45 - 11:10 AM**	

National Law School of India University, Bangalore
&
TMT Law Practice, New Delhi
Round table conference on
"Commercialization and Privatization of Outer Space: Issues for National Space Legislation"

DATE: 18TH JULY 2015
VENUE: ALLEN & OVERY CONFERENCE HALL, 2ND FLOOR, TRAINING CENTRE, NLSIU,
BANGALORE

PROGRAMME SCHEDULE

MEDIA PARTNER

WITNESS
INDIA'S FIRST MAGAZINE ON LEGAL AND CORPORATE AFFAIRS
www.witnessmag.in

PLENARY ADDRESS 11:10AM – 11:40AM
"National Space Legislation: What International Law Demands and How It Is Implemented"

PROF. (DR.) STEPHAN HOBE
Director, Institute of Air and Space Law, University of Cologne, Germany;
Jean Monnet Chair for International &European Law,
University of Cologne, Germany.

SESSION I: VOICE OF ACADEMIA & ATTORNEY 11:40 - 1:30 PM
CHAIRED BY: PROF. (DR.) V. BALAKISTA REDDY

Commercialisation of Remote Sensing and Geo-Spatial Data: Emerging Legal Challenges.	Prof. (Dr) V. Balakista Reddy Registrar, NALSAR and Head, Centre for Air and Space Law; Coordinator, M.K. Nambyar SAARC Law Centre, NALSAR, Hyderabad.
Potentials of Private Sector Participation in the Indian Space Sector: Policy and Legal Needs.	Prof. K. R. Sridhara Murthi Vice-President, International Institute of Space Law; Director, IIAEM, Jain University; Adjunct Faculty, National Institute of Advanced Studies, Bangalore; Former Managing Director, Antrix Corporation Ltd.
State Responsibility for the Space Activities of Private Actors	Dr. G. S. Sachdeva Wing Commander (Retd.), Indian Air Force and Adjunct Professor, Space Law.
A National Space Law for India: Deconstructing the Proposition	Dr. RanjanaKaul Partner, Dua Associates.
Key Elements in the National Space Legislation for India.	Dr Sandeepa Bhat Associate Professor and Coordinator, Forum for Air and Space Law & PGDASL, The WB National University of Juridical Sciences, Kolkata.
State Practices to National Space Legislation.	Mr. Kumar Abhijeet Assistant Professor, NLSIU, B'lore.

National Law School of India University, Bangalore
&
TMT Law Practice, New Delhi
Round table conference on
"Commercialization and Privatization of Outer Space: Issues for National Space Legislation"
DATE: 18TH JULY 2015
VENUE: ALLEN & OVERY CONFERENCE HALL, 2ND FLOOR, TRAINING CENTRE, NLSIU, BANGALORE

MEDIA PARTNER
WITNESS

PROGRAMME SCHEDULE

Lunch Break 1:30PM – 2:30 PM

SESSION II: VOICE OF PRIVATE SPACE PLAYERS 2:30 - 4:00 PM CHAIRED BY: PROF. K. R. SRIDHARAMURTHI	
Commercialisation of Outer Space: India's Perspective	Mr. D. S. Govindarajan President, Aniara Communications Pvt. Ltd.
The Indian Space Policy: Inclusion of Private Players and Acknowledgement of IP	Mr. Amitava Chakraborty Senior Consultant, TMT Law Practice, New Delhi.
A Manifesto for the Privatisation of the PSLV Production, Operation and Marketing.	Dr. Susmita Mohanty CEO, Earth2Orbit (E2O), www.earth2orbit.com
Creating a Policy Roadmap for the Commercial Space Activities.	Mr. Ashok G.V. Advocate and Managing Partner, CorLit Legal.
Space Laws around the World and Their Impact on Market and Industry.	Mr. Prashant Butani Senior Analyst, Northern Sky Research.
Space Law for Space Commerce or ViceVersa: A Chicken-and-Egg Situation for Space Commerce in India?'	Mr. Narayan Prasad Director, Spacecraft Systems, Dhruv Space Pvt. Ltd.

Tea Break 4:00PM - 4:15 PM

National Law School of India University, Bangalore
&
TMT Law Practice, New Delhi
Round table conference on
"Commercialization and Privatization of Outer Space: Issues for National Space Legislation"

DATE: 18TH JULY 2015
VENUE: ALLEN & OVERY CONFERENCE HALL, 2ND FLOOR, TRAINING CENTRE, NLSIU,

BANGALORE

PROGRAMME SCHEDULE

MEDIA PARTNER

WITNESS

SESSION III: OPEN HOUSE DISCUSSION 4:15 - 5:30 PM
CHAIRED BY: DR. RANJANA KAUL

Discussants: Invited Speakers, Guests and Faculty, NLSIU

Hon'ble Dr. M. Y. S. Prasad
Former Director, Satish Dhawan Space Centre (SHAR), Sriharikota, ISRO and Chairman, National Space Law Committee of ISRO.

Mr. K. Krishna
Vice President and Chief Technology Officer, Hughes Communications India Ltd.

Mr. Sunil Kumar
Senior Adviser, Science & Innovation, India; UK Science & Innovation Network, British Deputy High Commission.

Dr. Malay Adhikari
PhD in Space Law, Centre for International Legal Studies, JNU, New Delhi; MPhil in Space Law, NALSAR Hyderabad; LLM in International Law; MSc in Physics.

Mr. Prateep Basu
Analyst, Northern Sky Research.

Mr. Pulkit Kanwar
Skywalker, Mission Operations, TeamIndus, Axiom Research Labs Pvt Ltd.

Mr. Deva Prasad,
Assistant Professor, NLSIU, B'lore.

Tea Break 5:30PM - 5:45 PM

VALEDICTORY SESSION 5:45 – 6:45 PM

Summation	**Mr . Abhishek Malhotra** Managing Partner, TMT Law Practice, New Delhi.
The Way Forward	**Prof. (Dr.) R. VenkataRao** Vice-Chancellor, NLSIU B'lore.
Address by the Guest of Honour	**Hon'ble (Dr.) M. Y. S. Prasad** Former Director, Satish Dhawan Space Centre (SHAR),Sriharikota, ISRO and Chairman, National Space Law Committee of ISRO.
Valedictory Address by the Chief Guest	**Hon'ble Mr. Justice Raghvendra S. Chauhan,** Judge, High Court of Karnataka.
Vote of Thanks	**Mr. Kumar Abhijeet** Assistant Professor, NLSIU B'lore, Conference Coordinator.

www.ingramcontent.com/pod-product-compliance
Lightning Source LLC
Chambersburg PA
CBHW021540260326
41914CB00001B/97